EVERYTHING IS PERSONAL

ADVANCE PRAISE FOR *EVERYTHING IS PERSONAL, NOTES ON NOW*

"An extraordinary work, remarkably and unflinchingly true to its author's powerful, instantly recognizable voice—full of wisdom and passion and fierce intelligence. For Laurie Stone, the world we live in now is personal—everything and everywhere in it is her and the immediate place of her being. There is great beauty in this brave book, right at the very heart of it."

Mikhail Iossel, author of *Notes from Cyberground*

"There are many excellent essays here, but the one I'm most excited by is 'The Clock,' which is admirably complicit, resistant to all manner of received wisdom, self-questioning, ferocious, and little short of revelatory. I am a besotted fan."

David Shields, author of *Reality Hunger*

"'Don't take it personally,' we say to soften the blow of some humiliation or rebuff. Laurie Stone shows why that is nonsense when it comes to the wounds of society. The great virtue of her book is that in it we encounter a lively, opinionated voice, full of brio, moxie and intelligence. "

Phillip Lopate, author of *A Mother's Tale*

"Laurie Stone believes in the power of pleasure, even in the darkest times. Free and freeing, clear and bright, a cyclone of history written by an acutely observing eye, *Everything Is Personal* makes radical social change and individual transformation seem not only necessary but inviting and funny. Laurie Stone has given us 'a place to live while the world learns to breathe again.'"

Joseph Keckler, author of *Dragon at the Edge of a Flat World*

"This book is a collection of the responses and reminiscences of a writer who, for decades, has been richly connected to the warmth and vibrancy of popular American culture: how it reads, plays, and protests our benighted political life. Savor it slowly, let the pleasure of its sensibility become absorbent: I recommend a few pages a night before bedtime."

Vivian Gornick, author of *The Odd Woman and the City*

ADVANCE PRAISE FOR *EVERYTHING IS PERSONAL, NOTES ON NOW*

"Stone knows that in a world crowded with opinions, a thought can't just be good, it has to be elegant. Her powerful sentences smile at their own precision, they don't just make a social point but offer a model on how to think, how to think in this time. As she says, 'About the matter of redemption, as far as I am concerned, human beings don't fall and therefore do not need to be redeemed. We are not on a path, period.'"

Michael Tolkin, author of *The Player*

"To read Laurie Stone's *Everything Is Personal, Notes On Now* is to read Laurie Stone, is to experience a present tense intimacy with a lusty, testy, ebullient, scintillating mind, a woman's mind, a woman who remembers the summer of '68 and is living, right now, in this instant, through the Trump years..."

Diane Seuss, author of *Four-Legged Girl*

EVERYTHING IS PERSONAL

NOTES ON NOW

Laurie Stone

Scuppernong Editions Greensboro 2020

First printing
ISBN 978-1-7329328-2-1

DESIGN. Text in Arno Pro. Titles in Avenir. Cover title in Eagle Bold. Cover and interior design by Andrew Saulters. Scuppernong Editions colophon by Rachel York.

Scuppernong Editions offers the occasional publication of adventuresome, commercially questionable writing in all genres.

Scuppernong Editions
304 South Elm Street
Greensboro, NC 27401

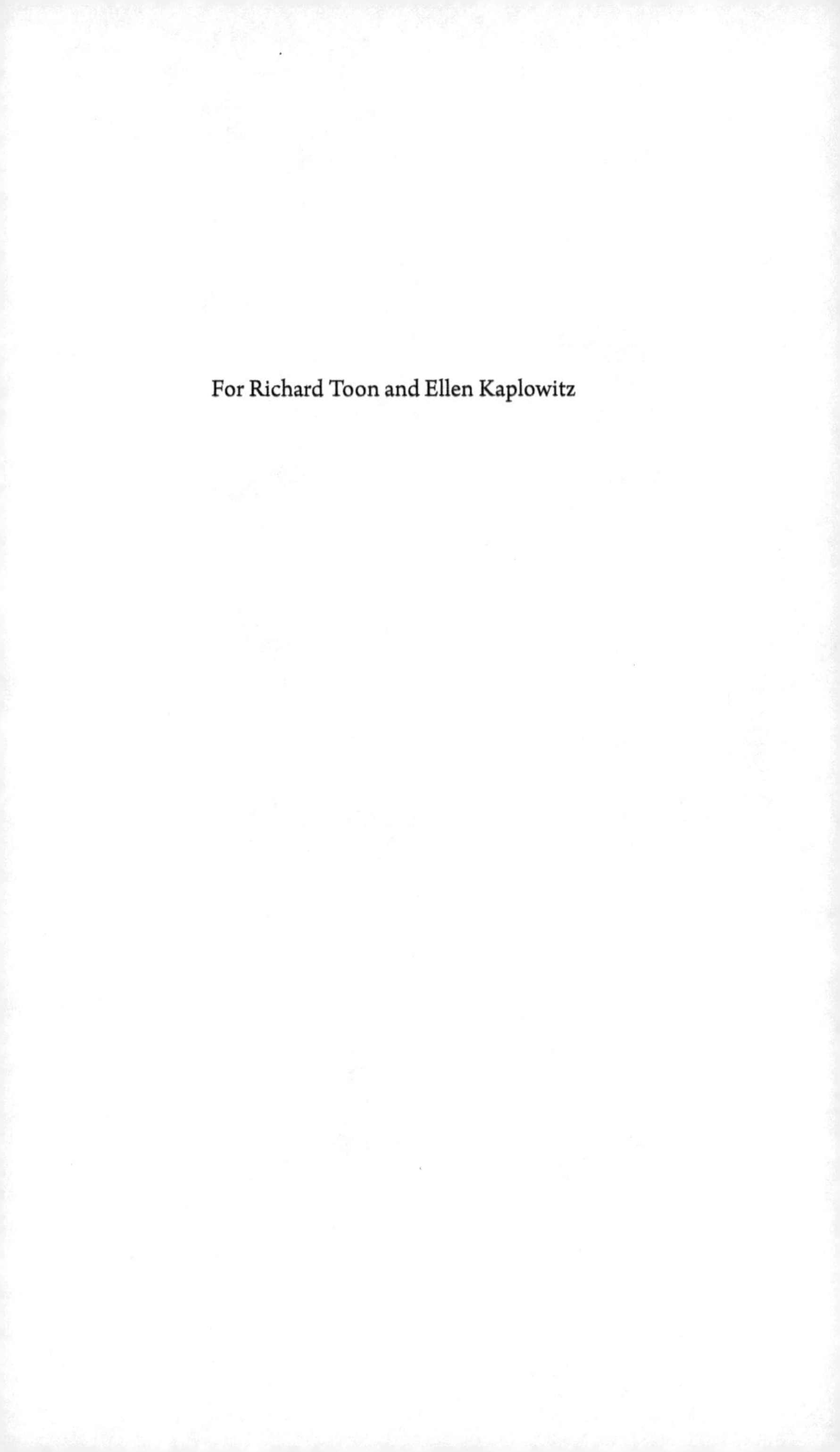

For Richard Toon and Ellen Kaplowitz

November 20, 2016.
Everything unimaginable happens eventually

EVERYTHING IS PERSONAL

Introduction by Chris Kraus *ix*

Aliveness 3
The Clock 7
Was It Good for You? 9
The Clock 23
Postcards from DC 41
The Clock 47
Body Language 49
The Clock 53
The Village Voice 71
The Clock 79
Valerie Solanas 8 Ways 81
The Clock 91
Personal Life 111
The Clock 135
In 1968 I Thought It Would Always Be 1968 159
The Clock 169
House 171

Afterword by Marco Roth 175
Acknowledgments 179
About the Author 181

ADAPTATION

An Introduction by Chris Kraus

"People get Darwin wrong," Laurie Stone writes on September 8, 2017 in her occasional Facebook diary. "It's not the ruthless that survive. It's the ones that adapt." And she would know. Born in 1946, Stone enjoyed a distinguished twenty-five year long career as a writer for the *Village Voice* before losing her job during an early wave of editorial purges. Once one of New York City's most august left/liberal cultural institutions, the paper no longer exists.

In 2006 Stone met the museological scholar Richard Toon during a writing residency at Yaddo. They fell in love, and eventually Stone left her home on the Upper West Side several months out of the year to join him in Scottsdale, Arizona where he was teaching at ASU. In Scottsdale, she and Toon devised a writing practice that began as a series of mutual prompts and Stone's critical voice started to shift towards something more time-based and open. She began writing (very) short stories, often in response to these prompts, in which the gaps between present and past, desire and truth are revealed like a series of lucid dreams, highly compressed into the moment of their recall. Some of these pieces were published in her 2016 story collection *My Life as an Animal.*

As a student at Barnard in the mid-1960s, Stone was awakened to feminism in Kate Millet's classes. She became a younger participant in second-wave radical feminist groups, absorbing all of their information. As a writer and citizen, she embraced what's now known as "intersectional feminism," writing, speaking, volunteering and demonstrating to advance human and environmental rights. The title of this essay collection, *Everything Is Personal, Notes From Now,* is a flip nod to radical feminism's most famous dictum. But the breadth of Stone's interests, her vision of what "the political" means is reflected in the range of the subjects discussed here. She writes about the seemingly equally unstoppable processes of aging and upstate New York's rural gentrification. She writes about mall walking. She condemns blatant abuses of gendered power while leaving plenty of room for the inexplicable contradictions of human desire. She defends comedy—"if comedy does not contain displaced anger, it won't be funny"—and reports from a Washington demonstration where she and thousands of others congregate in the halls of the US Senate to bird-dog legislators during the Brett Kavanaugh Supreme Court confirmation hearings.

While Stone is mindful that the activism she engaged in decades before achieved quantifiable results—Nixon resigned, abortion was legalized, LGBQT rights were gained—she refuses to see the outcome of the Kavanaugh hearings as an utter defeat. Back in New York, she feels "less something, having gone. What's the word? Passive? Done to? … I thought about those giant white buildings, humming with power like an engine turning over. You have to put your belongings on a scanner to get in, but you can get in. … All the people in those buildings moving along, their faces aloof, trying to ignore us, unable to ignore us … We reversed the gaze, and it felt like the opposite of despair."

In this volume, Stone reinvents herself as a critic. Deprived of a platform that no longer exists, she decides to use her Facebook page as a kind of moral and intellectual diary. That is, she adapts. I'm in awe of the nerve and courage it must have taken to do this. In its decades-long heyday, the *Village Voice* was a bastion of critical taste. Artists looked to its writers for validation, and its writers wielded an enviable amount of judgment and power. But it's through this adaptation that Stone arrives at a new, more modest and human—which is to say, more effective and timely—critical form. The pieces in "The

Clock" all began as posts on her personal page. They combine the observational discipline, presence and sense of breath that characterize Stone's writings in *My Life As An Animal* with her love of argumentation and her acute sense of reason. Her beloved sister Ellen dies over the course of these entries. Stone mourns her sister, buys a pair of flip-flops in Scottsdale during a rain storm, reconsiders the Polanski film *Rosemary's Baby*, goes to Amsterdam, sleepwalks, reads Peter Handke. In the wake of her grief over personal and cultural losses, Stone becomes a critical monologist, and at times, a stand-up comedian. She basks in ambivalence. Her essays move freely between subjects and there are times when the argument stops and the text simply breathes.

On May 7, 2017 she writes: "I am alone in Arizona, where I am seldom alone. Time feels larger here, like a vast desert filled with dusty vegetation. I am pretending I am a mayfly, and this day is my entire life ... I am reading several books at the same time and picking up items I want to pack even though I can't pack the light conditions and the pinkness of air you see only in Arizona."

In Paris during the German Occupation, Michel Leiris wrote in his personal diary, "June 6, 1941 ... Life feels smothered, dampened, as if under a bushel or behind a mask. Impression of fog, penetrating to the point of liquefaction. Like a light but persistent rain, which the sky will never clear itself of, time passes."

On July 25, 2019, Stone writes the Facebook post that will retrospectively define the rest of this book:

"On November 8, 2016, the US experienced a fascist coup. Hillary didn't lose the election. There was no election. All the sentences spilled in the interim explain nothing, reveal nothing, express nothing true about what has happened and why it happened. The analysis is sawdust and unreadable. ... Looking for origins is reverse teleology. The thing you are talking about as a thing is mutating all the time..."

Stone is engaging, sharp, funny throughout these pages but no matter how far she ranges, she holds onto the recognition that daily life in the US is being lived under a dark cloud. She makes the stakes very clear. Her "Notes on Now" are completely illuminating.

EVERYTHING IS PERSONAL

ALIVENESS

The night of the election I met a friend at the apartment of friends of hers, and we watched the terrifying numbers tick along the screen. The TV was enormous, which made the numbers look more ominous. This friend was beautiful and had immigrated to the US from a country allied with the former Soviet Union. She worked for an organization that protects people from artistic and political censorship, and we didn't have words for what we felt. The next day I flew from New York to Phoenix to see Richard and drink at night to dull the way aliveness felt.

A friend recently died I wish I could talk to. In the past, when I went out onto the streets with her to protest, it felt like we were in conversation with a government, however repugnant its policies. We thought we could produce change, and we did. Johnson decided not to run again. Nixon resigned. Abortion became a legal right. Affirmative action changed hiring practices. Gay people were included in policies against discrimination. Now, marching feels like running the old game with the old rules when none of this exists anymore. It feels like accepting some kind of framework where oligarchic feudal terrorism is considered a government and we stand for that government's tolerance of protest. I kind of know what my friend would say. She'd say, "I see your point, darling, but we have to do it anyway," and then she would sigh one of her luxurious, *Weltschmerz* sighs.

Richard and I are buying a house outside the town of Hudson. The town was the home of Mahican people before Europeans entered the scene in the seventeenth century. New England whalers from Nantucket and Martha's Vineyard settled there in the nineteenth century, and in the early part of the twentieth century, it was a hub for gambling and prostitution. In the 1970s and 1980s, empty storefronts with dusty chairs, withered plants, and other remnants of tragic departures alternated with antiques stores run mainly by gay men and women. These days a pound of salami on the high street costs $32.

I know this because Richard was having low sugar and needed something to eat, so I wandered into a market on Warren Street to buy him stuff for a sandwich. The clerk told me the price of salami with a strangled voice. I didn't mention it was about the same price as two ounces of silver. A shiny metal. A stuffed tube of meat and fat. A sizable population of African Americans has for generations lived in a section of Hudson close to the river. The value of their houses has no doubt shot up now that they are proximate to a string of expensive hotels that have the glossy, fern-bar look of *boîtes* in Tribeca. Still, we need to live somewhere while the world is falling apart.

Today we bought an air conditioner from a woman in our building on the Upper West Side of Manhattan. Her husband had died and she was forgoing her lovely, rent-stabilized bastion to follow her brother's advice and move to Chandler, Arizona, where she would likely cook to a crisp and die of loneliness in the absence of street life. The next day we passed her walking, and she looked worried. I said, "What's wrong?" She said, "Oy, the packing." I said, "What if you don't like it there?" She said, "I have to like it there." She was a certain age and thought she needed to lean against a man. I know how old I am by looking in other people's eyes. It's subtle at first. You think you are talking to a peer, and suddenly you can see they don't know who they are talking to, and they become polite and soft around the edges, as if they might wound you. The only thing that wounds is isolation.

My friend who died spent her life working for a more just world. Really, every waking minute. She organized scores of people for each action she dreamed up. She was able to accomplish so much because she didn't answer the phone and didn't watch TV. I look at my phone so much my head is permanently angled downward. Also, right now, I have a reason to live because Season 7 of *The Great British Baking Show* is starting soon.

On the day after the November 2016 election, the writer Mikhail Iossel posted a message on Facebook that has stayed with me. Misha lives in Montreal now. Having grown up a Jew in the former Soviet Union, he thought these words would help us: "America has proven unable to resist the virus of fascism currently abroad in the Western world. Let's hope its political institutions will turn out to be resilient enough to conquer it from within over the next four years. Difficult times are ahead, but America must hang in there. This is how we used to live back in the Soviet Union: Rely upon the people you love, upon your circle of close friends, don't talk about politics with strangers, assume that people you don't know may well be, and likely are, possessed by the hateful totalitarian Soviet mindset; try not to watch much of anything other than sports or non-political movies and art concerts on television; read books, write, have drinks with friends, look at the sky, dream of a better tomorrow. Hang in there. You still have the potent option of the free elections we did not have back there. This is not the end of the world, even if it may feel that way right now. America is stronger than its temporary madness. In the end, we'll be all right."

Does this post bring tears to your eyes? It does mine. For one thing, he was wrong about our institutions being forceful enough to rout the other side's illegalities and lies. Also, we don't have free elections. We have each other, though, and a world we desperately love. The friend with whom I watched the election results is fighting harder than ever to protect free expression and the right to your own vocabulary as more and more people of all political stripes try to revise what you say. In a sense this book is one long comment in appreciation of Misha's post.

For the past decade or so, I've been trying out writing on Facebook, posting fiction stories, memoir narratives, social commentary, and art criticism. I often think of the posts as postcards, written from nowhere in particular and addressed to everyone. The longer pieces I have gone on to form from these posts have been enlarged by the interactive nature of social media and the comments people have made. I don't debate ideas on my posts or in life because I don't think people convince other people to change their minds. I think we learn through exposure to new information, measured against our own experience. We change because staying in the same painful, worn-out state is too much to bear.

Richard and I have a little practice we exchange in the morning. We list three things in the moment we love. It was invented to subvert the human tendency to suck on misery and dread. In this moment, I love Feminism: The Reboot, ushered in via the post-Trump #MeToo movement. I love the interaction of Facebook, even though it exploits us and can kill us slowly or quickly. I love my sister, who died while I was writing these pieces, and whom I search for these days when I look in the mirror.

THE CLOCK

November 11, 2017. In the wake of revelations about Louis C.K., I'm concerned masturbation is getting a bad rap.

WAS IT GOOD FOR YOU?

On the #MeToo movement and the freedom to circulate

The other day I read a story by Paul Bowles in *Points in Time* (1982), set in Morocco, where Bowles lived. The story takes place 150 years in the past and concerns a Jewish girl who marries into the family of a Muslim man who is smitten by her beauty. In order to marry him, she must convert to Islam. Shortly after the marriage, she realizes she has made a mistake. She is made the servant of the other female members of the family and told she cannot leave the house.

Bowles writes: "When she remonstrated with Mohammed [her husband], saying she needed to go out for a walk in the fresh air, he answered that it was common knowledge that a woman goes out only three times during her life: Once when she is born and leaves her mother's womb, once when she marries and leaves her father's house, and once when she dies and leaves this world. He advised her to walk on the roof like other women."

She decides to leave. Her husband is shamed. She is captured as an infidel and beheaded.

The story made me think about many things, including the beauty and threat of *circulation* as a concept and about the many calls we are hearing, many in contradictory contexts, for things and people to be removed from circulation. Among them are objects, such as the Confederate flag, called on to be removed from public spaces and relocated in museums. Calls for the work of certain male artists accused of sexual aggressions, such as Roman Polanski, to be deposited in archives and banned from public viewing. Calls for certain male performers, professors, writers, and editors, accused of offensive statements and behaviors, such as Lorin Stein, fired last year as editor of *The Paris Review* for sexual harassment, to be removed from their jobs.

The desire to nail whatever bastard you can get your hands on as puny reparation for thousands of years of unpunished male violence has been driving #MeToo usefully and buoyantly since the election of Trump. #MeToo is not exactly a movement, and it's not exactly organized. It was the name devised in 2006 by Tarana Burke to spark consciousness of sexual violence against women of color, and there's an undeniable whiff of racism in the way the concept didn't fly off the shelves until the majority culture got behind it. That and the general sense of powerlessness people felt after the crazily unfair defeat of Hillary. #MeToo has generally been depicted as Feminism: The Reboot, as it has gone about raising consciousness, like a giant leaf blower gathering dessicated scoundrels. These are the men, protected by handlers and money, who say to women, "Let me feel you up, let me fuck you, and, although I will make you feel like a worthless worm, I can make you rich and successful."

This is ordinary sexism, a word too small, it seems, for the colossus of hate-mongering and abuse it must carry on its bony shoulders. The women's movement had been documenting the uninvited gropes and threatening mind games of male humans for 50 years, but it took a stolen election by a massive criminal with proud contempt for women to make feminism—or a version of feminism—palatable even to men. As each rodent has gone down, he's squeaked, "This is business as usual. You've changed the rules! I call foul." For the first time in a concerted way there are hairy consequences.

#MeToo has managed to reveal slime-as-usual practices in worlds that have pretended to be prettier than they are, among them the academy, broadcasting, and publishing. But #MeToo risks diverting its momentum with fuzzy thinking, and I want to focus on this here, in hopes of expanding the attention of the movement beyond the terrible things done to women of a sexual nature to other terrible things done to them, in hopes of moving beyond the acts of individuals to the gender biases in institutions, among them religions.

#MeToo is thrilling when it exposes criminals and predators. It is chilling, however, when the target of a #MeToo campaign—for lack of a better term—has committed no crime or readily identifiable harm and has, rather, caused offense, or rattled some people, or triggered them, or made them feel an emotion they didn't want to feel. Sometimes the emotion is arousal, but let's put that aside for a moment. We need to look more carefully at category mistakes and keep in mind whether a call for punishment or decirculation in the name of feminism actually expands—or crimps—freedom for women. Here are some categories that ask us to think about *circulation*. The list is not exhaustive.

Objects that symbolize harm and spread harm

Confederate flags and Confederate monuments come to mind. These objects, celebrating the haters of the past and authorizing the hatred of racists now, have no place in public space, the way swastikas have no place in public space. What to do with them once they are collected? That's the messy question. Document and destroy them? Install them in museums, as if museums and archives are places where objects and ideas can go to die? As if museums can speed the process of detaching these artifacts from social relevance? They can't. Museums and archives are not going to drain the poison from cultural wares, nor should they be tasked with the job.

Counter examples are concentration camps and slave quarters as museums, which preserve the history of the oppressed rather than memorializing the accomplishments of those in power. Perhaps in our cultural moment we want histories that only express points of view from under the boot. Here's to new kinds of museums with no obligation to established power that will want to assume this responsibility.

People who have committed crimes of violence against females and continue to make art

In 1977, Roman Polanski was charged with rape by use of drugs of a thirteen-year-old girl. He pled guilty to a lesser charge of "unlawful sexual intercourse" and fled the US. As repulsive and cruel as these acts are, my feeling is this: Punish the artist and leave the art alone. Banning art does not look good on a movement, ever. Theoretically, even if a Confederate monument existed that you could classify as art, it, too, might call for a particular form of display and explanatory label text. To my knowledge, this object does not exist.

When you learn discomfiting facts about a person, you can't look at their work the same way as before. It messes with your head, and you may feel so turned off you don't want to engage with it further. You could also find yourself turned off by work made by a person who did not do bad things. For example, I have always loved the work of Ricky Gervais, but right now he's on my shit list because he makes a loud point of referring to the worst people he can think of as *cunts*. Ricky thinks there is nothing more debased in existence than female genitalia, and to that I say, "Go fuck yourself." (Have you noticed that only women are expected to laugh at insults?). Still, I will probably watch his next Netflix performance, while publicly expressing my problem with him.

If you continue to engage with the work of an artist who has done bad things, what you have learned will produce a new reading of their work. It has to. At the same time, you can't judge the work itself only by the qualities of the person who made it. Bad people make good art. Turning away from a work of art or the artist who made it is a personal choice. Advocating for its removal from circulation is a social choice. The motive is partly to punish the artist. *Don't let them earn more money and acclaim, since they are bad,* the thinking goes. Some also argue that a work of art made by a person who does bad things contaminates the culture. This last notion is more contaminating of a culture than any work of art could be.

Art, for the most part, is more complex and mysterious than the person who made it. That's why it needs to remain in circulation. Polanski's *Rosemary's Baby* is a perfect case in point, steered as it is by Polanski's wit and identification with the targeted and isolated Rosemary. No more *Rosemary's Baby* produces a duller, more shriveled world.

Some people argue that removing the art of men who do bad things to women will make more space for the work of women and minority artists. Nice sentiment, but that's not how art works in the world. There isn't a fixed-sized art pie, i.e., a smaller piece of production for you guarantees a bigger piece of art pie for me. Art moves in and out of fashion, sure, and the work of male artists has been more supported than the work of female artists, but removing the art of men is not going to help female directors get jobs, and it will not benefit the cause of freedom for women.

Firing men who do bad things to women or who promote men who do bad things to women

I say fire away—if the men are criminals or prove themselves unfit for the job. Ian Buruma fits this description. He was fired as editor of *The New York Review of Books* for publishing a self-serving defense (with unchecked false statements) by Jian Ghomeshi, a man publicly accused of physical and sexual brutality by nearly 20 women, including one charge of overcoming a woman's resistance by choking. Ghomeshi was acquitted at his trial, but Buruma made the wrong bet about the times he was living in, believing that Ghomeshi would be seen as a victim of social media mob action rather than a serial abuser who got off without a jail sentence.

This is what Buruma said to Isaac Chotiner in a *Slate* interview about his reasons for publishing the Ghomeshi self-defense: "I'm no judge of the rights and wrongs of every allegation. How can I be? All I know is that in a court of law he was acquitted, and there is no proof he committed a crime. The exact nature of his behavior—how much consent was involved—I have no idea, nor is it really my concern. My concern is what happens to somebody who has not been found guilty in any criminal sense but who perhaps deserves social opprobrium, but how long should that last, what form it should take, etc."

I have to say, the comment that grabs me by the pussy is this: "The exact nature of his behavior . . . I have no idea, nor is it really my concern." Whoa. Why is it not your concern since you gave him space to lie about it in your paper? All the things Buruma cares about are valid to care about regarding moral opprobrium and term limits on shunning, but not caring about what the man actually did and the women he did it to? Bye, bye.

Deposing men who do creepy and humiliating sexual things to women that are not crimes

I have devised this category for Louis C.K., although others no doubt belong here as well. In November 2017, Louis admitted to asking women who came to his hotel rooms if he could masturbate in front of them. He gained their consent. These women wanted to work with him professionally, and the ones who stayed felt they had to watch him jerk off as part of the deal. Louis said in a public statement he was sorry. After his admission, he was fired from his current jobs. A film he was in was shelved. And past episodes of his TV show *Louie* remain unavailable for streaming.

In August 2018, he made an unannounced appearance at a comedy club in NYC. The next day, on Facebook, a female writer weighed in that he had not sufficiently "redeemed" himself to get back on stage. I was struck by the peculiarly Christian concept of *redemption* coming into play in a case like this, and I was reminded of the long fissure in the women's movement dividing women who see their role as moral reformers and women who advocate for the sexual liberation of all people. I place myself firmly in the second camp. About the matter of *redemption,* as far as I am concerned, human beings don't fall and therefore do not need to be redeemed.

We are not on a path with an ideal narrative arc of right living. We are not on a path, period.

Causing someone to look at your penis is a form of flashing. In private, though, it's something people do all the time in ordinary sex, so the category of taking out your penis in your own hotel room isn't actionable in itself. The room was not a public space. Louis flashed women who wanted to be in his orbit. They didn't work for him, so legally it's not sexual harassment. He wanted to see them squirm or submit as part of his excitement. He was a shit.

How long does he remain out of circulation? Is he ever allowed to earn money again as a writer and performer? Some people have argued his future earnings should fund the women he grossed out and other art projects by women. Maybe he will direct some money that way, out of a sense of obligation or positive public relations, rather the way after the Valdez, Alaska oil spill, Exxon paid for animal rehab facilities there.

Some people have argued that Louis's appearance at the comedy club wasn't announced and that those in the audience therefore had no choice but to see him—another instance of whipping it out, as it were. It was argued that his premature return trivialized the harm he had caused the women he coerced and, in a sense, all women who have been harassed.

Indeed, you can see his appearance as a form of aggression, but there is also a tradition in comedy clubs of unannounced sets by stars trying out new work. In clubs, too, if you don't like an act, you can walk out and come back. You're not in lockdown. What people who complained meant is they wanted a trigger warning, even though comedy is the thing that lampoons trigger warnings and other forms of pre-emptive protection. Comedy is the thing that is supposed to take you hostage and unteach you how to feel scared. If you feel comfortable and safe in a comedy club, you are at some other kind of performance.

I don't find sexist humor funny because the power position in comedy is the place of no power. Louis knows this some of the time, the way we all do. He can switch moods in startling ways, slipping between hilarity, embarrassment, failure, and yearning. Will he have anything to say that can move us if he passes over what happened to him? I think he could turn his experience into a subject for comedy if he were willing to struggle with it. How was he feeling when he flashed his cock at unsuspecting women? What did the looks on their faces tell him? How does he feel about the impact of all this on his daughters? To make this funny, he would have to put himself in the position he placed women in without portraying himself as a victim. A man like Louis, who thinks very hard about comic sources, should be able to do this.

Louis is an artist, who wants to work. His art is interactive, and he's got to show up somewhere, at some point. Some people have argued, No, he doesn't have to show up anywhere. He has occupied enough real estate in the zeitgeist. I say to that, Well, I don't want to see a single person in the GOP and most Democrats appear in public, but I don't think you are going to help me out with that.

You want to tell Louis about the pain his actions have caused? Tell him. Maybe he will hear you. You don't like him? Don't go see him. If you don't like the films of Roman Polanski and Woody Allen, don't see them, either. If you don't like the people who fund their work, boycott them and protest outside theaters. You may be a minority voice, but it's the way cultural change happens, not through banning artistic expression. How to help women speak publicly against abuse without being consigned to the role of scold or gravitating toward it? Through comedy, would be my bet.

Firing men who blunder publicly in ways that are difficult to categorize, in the name of feminism

On November 26, 2018, the day film director Bernardo Bertolucci died, the film critic David Edelstein posted on Facebook: "Even grief goes better with butter." The quip captioned a still from *Last Tango in Paris*, depicting Marlon Brando atop a prone Maria Schneider. It's from the scene in which Brando's character anally rapes Schneider's character, using butter as lube. Schneider's face is anguished, and her fists are balled up.

On November 27, the NPR show *Fresh Air,* where Edelstein worked as a contributor, issued this statement: "Today we learned about film critic David Edelstein's Facebook post in response to the death of film director Bernardo Bertolucci. The post is offensive and unacceptable, especially given actress Maria Schneider's experience during the filming of *Last Tango in Paris.* The post does not meet the standards that we expect from *Fresh Air* contributors, or from film journalists associated with WHYY NPR. We appreciate the apology David posted, but we have decided to end *Fresh Air*'s association with him, and have informed David accordingly."

Here is some background on Edelstein's use of the word *butter.* Because in the film butter is used as lube, butter became a sex joke from the movie's 1973 premiere on. I saw Edelstein's post and thought, Wow, that's really tone deaf and dumb. I remembered reading about Schneider's 2007 interview with the *Daily Mail,* where she described Bertolucci's treatment of her during the filming of *Last Tango.* Writing in *The Washington Post* on November 26, 2018, Elahe Izadi lays out what happened during filming and the repercussions of those events, drawing on accounts by Schneider, Brando, and Bertolucci.

I summarize: Brando and Bertolucci were having breakfast before the filming of the rape scene and together devised the notion of using butter. They didn't inform Schneider, who was 19 at the time. The rape was in the script, but not the butter. She did not know she could have called her agent and refused to perform something not in the script. She says her tears in the scene were real. After the movie, unprepared for the degree of public scrutiny she experienced, she used drugs and attempted suicide. She died of cancer in 2011.

In 2013, during a filmed interview, Bertolucci said he purposely withheld the use of the butter because: "I wanted her reaction as a girl, not as an actress. I wanted her to react humiliated." He said Schneider hated him for the rest of her life and that he felt guilty toward her. In interviews Brando also said he had felt humiliated by Bertolucci. It was cold during the shooting of his one, full frontal nude scene, and his parts shrank. The scene was later scrapped. Schneider said she thought Bertolucci was in love with Brando and that originally her role was supposed to be played by a boy. Amid the ferment of #MeToo, Bertolucci's manipulation of Schneider was revisited and widely condemned.

The association of butter and anal sex is not a problem for me now or in the past. Anal sex is about sex. The problem for me is not that a fictional scene depicted anal rape. The problem is what we now know about Schneider's experience at the hands of Bertolucci. This is what bears on Edelstein's remark. Another thing. The reason butter became a sex joke has to do not with the anal rape of Schneider's character but with a later scene. Brando's character says to Schneider's character, "Get the butter," because he wants her to finger him anally, and she does. When I saw *Last Tango* in 1973, people had more to say about the second scene than the first, and this speaks to the times. A girl gets raped, oh yeah, that happens. A guy gets penetrated, even though he asks for it, well that spurred all kinds of anxious and titillated homocurious responses. It was also as if a generation of boys and girls, raised to have vanilla sex, were invited to a better party.

After Edelstein posted his quip, people on social media instantly let him know the joke was a bomb. The reason it bombed is that it made Schneider the target. It trashed her, given her experience with Bertolucci. It trashed all women who have been slimed sexually and emotionally by older men in the name of art. It insulted all women who have been slimed sexually and emotionally in the name of nothing but freewheeling sadism. So that would include all of us.

On November 28, Andrew O'Hehir wrote a piece in *Salon* about Edelstein's firing, in which he outlined attacks on the film critic, most influentially and sternly by actor Martha Plimpton. Plimpton reposted Edelstein's bad joke on Twitter, calling for his firing and saying she had avoided any mention of Bertolucci's death "precisely because of this moment in which a sexual assault of an actress was intentionally captured on film." In fact, as Elahe Izadi makes clear, Schneider alleged no actual rape or "sexual assault" in her account. She felt violated by being excluded from decisions about the rape scene, and she felt keenly the manipulation Bertolucci had engineered. O'Hehir asks, "Does it make it all better if we conclude that Edelstein was making light of a fictional rape, or a fictional incident that might be rape? Definitely not, as he has acknowledged. Furthermore, it's baffling that a person so deeply immersed in movies and media either didn't know or had forgotten about Schneider's comments, and Bertolucci's subsequent half-apology."

After Edelstein deleted his original post, he wrote again on Facebook on the same day: "Regarding Bertolucci's death, I made a stupid joke here on my FB page that turns out to have been beyond stupid—grotesque. The first and only time I ever saw *Last Tango* was in 1977. I remembered the scene in question as part of a consensual, increasingly S&M relationship that ends with the woman being forced to shoot the man. I didn't remember it as a rape and I didn't know the real-life story about Maria Schneider. The line was callous and wrong even if it HAD been consensual, but given that it wasn't I'm sick at the thought of how it read and what people logically conclude about me. I have never and would never make light of rape, in fiction or in reality."

Let's pause for a moment. Isn't there always a way to make a joke about something if you can figure out how to frame it? I think there is. The sanctimony of Edelstein's mea culpa has the same tenor as the sanctimony in rebukes of him. How about we ditch all sanctimony. It's not that feminism can't take a joke. It's that jokes involving feminism beat up people who have already been beaten up. There could have been a way to make excellent cracks about Brando's cold-weather weenie and Bertolucci's crush on him and include butter, had Edelstein thought in these terms, and there's the rub. In that inattention lies the ease of trivializing everything that is not you—in Edelstein's case a straight white male—and it's breathed like air.

In a saner social moment, when taking offense was not actionable, Edelstein would have received a reprimand and been offered clear guidelines about the acceptable content of his posts on social media. His firing is an example of what I have taken to calling "sensitivity harassment." Words can hurt, but to censor them and fire the people who use them has a far more chilling effect on our society than social interaction with these moments. What should be the reach of organizations to police the speech of employees when they are not on the job? How do you feel about a dismissal on the grounds of unspecified moral standards? How do you feel about an organization speaking for feminism when its real aim is to cover its ass for fear of pushback or simply to clean house of an otherwise bothersome employee? What specifically feminist positions and understandings does NPR expect from its contributors? I would really like to see these spelled out.

What offends you is always going to be my endangered devotion, and vice versa. You believe in God and want me to believe in God, for example. I believe religions promote gender discrimination. I don't even want the power to make you stop believing what you believe for this reason: Repression and moral opprobrium from all political stances serve power and money. Power wants a populace that is frightened to dissent, whose members are in seeming lockstep agreement, and who will police each other so repression becomes internalized and reflexive. Then you have people you can control and sell ideas and things to. My first concept for this piece was to convene a round table of views on Edelstein. A surprising number of people I queried told me they did not want to risk placing themselves in the line of fire on social media.

A society becomes changed not by fiat but when outmoded ways of thinking are tossed into dusty corners and forgotten, like the lives of millions of women and girls in the actual world, who have been destroyed because their existences caused offense. Nothing can be cleansed, and among things considered contaminants might be your ideas or mine. The ideas of feminists are among the first things to be erased when waves of social cleansing are enforced. That's why, from a practical perspective, it's a terrible idea for women to line up with censorship.

Everything exciting and challenging in the world is a mixture of terror and pleasure. Some sort of sexual feeling or erotic response or negative erotic response is part of every interaction we have with other people of all ages and even other animals throughout our lives. Let's not pretend otherwise as a way to simplify our conversations about abuse, rape, harassment, and other unwanted attention that takes a sexual or erotic form. Seeking safety may be the most dangerous thing we can do. There will never be a solid, agreed-upon notion of safety, and I don't want to be protected from what you think it's bad for me to know or do.

When you hear about another white, tone-deaf man losing his job because he caused offense, you do not need to care about the man. You need to care about the issue of circulation and things being denied that right. The circulation of the female body in public space, unguarded by male protection and permission to move, is among the most transformative social actions in the world.

THE CLOCK

December 5, 2016. Last night I watched several chunks of *The Clock* (2010), the great film collage created by Christian Marclay. The movie is a loop that lasts 24 hours and consists of thousands of film clips depicting a watch or a clock that characters look at in a scene. The images are assembled so that time moves forward in the shots as it does in real time for the viewer, and the effect is extraordinarily compelling. Partly it's the pleasure of recognizing amusing or famous scenes that have been inscribed in our collective memory, such as footage of Harold Lloyd dangling by the hands of a giant clock over an abyss of space that separates him from the street below and certain death. It's a brilliant silent comedy. In one sequence when it looks as though Lloyd will climb to safety, his foot gets caught in a spring he can't escape. In part the film is thrilling because it's unendingly suspenseful without resolution. Will it happen? Will we meet? Is there time to get there? Many of the scenes take place at train stations and airport lounges, the bardo spaces we occupy between movements from point A to point B. The film is a heart-tugging ode to waiting. Waiting for death, ultimately. Time is always about death. And once we evolved to our final understanding that human life exists outside teleological meaning—we're not characters in a narrative that has been thought out and designed—all that was left for us was the contemplation of beauty. The film celebrates beauty in the cracks, and while we contemplate beauty we forget for those moments the station where the train we are on will ultimately arrive.

Richard and I first saw parts of the film in 2010, where it was shown at the Venice Biennale we attended. We saw other parts when it was shown at MOMA in New York City. On both occasions, we felt it was the best kind of drug, and we couldn't get enough.

February 22, 2017. My mother was a racist. During the last three years of her life, following a stroke, she came to share her apartment with people of color. Her aides were mostly women from Caribbean countries, plus several white women and a gay man. Day after day from the moment she awoke to the time she closed her eyes, she was in the hands of other people. She loved them, not all equally, but love was in the room. She taught her aides Yiddish. They taught her Jamaican slang. She shared her bed when they piled on to watch TV. She kissed their hands. She became a human being right before she was no longer anything but a comic memory to her aides, who nine years later still talk to each other and to my sister and me about how they taught her to be a person.

April 22, 2017. Charlotte Brontë was born on this day 201 years ago. The heroines her sisters created were beautiful, so in the spirit of a dare, Charlotte wrote *Jane Eyre,* in which a plain, orphaned governess wins the heart of a rogue addicted to beautiful women.

The novel was published in 1847 and was an immediate rage. The intimate voice of the storyteller made people feel she was speaking directly to them. Charlotte, not Dickens, invented the child narrator who acutely registers pain. Before publication, Charlotte's editors urged her to tone down the harshness of the opening chapters, set at Lowood School, and to temper the agonizing death of Helen Burns (based on the death of Charlotte's older sister Elizabeth). She refused.

A decade earlier, she'd sought encouragement from Robert Southey, then England's Poet Laureate, who told her women should not write. After the publication of *Jane Eyre,* she mentioned to her father she had written a novel, that it had earned praising reviews, and that she was making money. Wearily, he said he might consider reading it.

After her marriage to a minister at the age of 38, Charlotte did not write much and died nine months later from a complicated pregnancy, but until that time and except for periods when she worked as a teacher or a governess, she lived at home with her siblings, and they wrote all the time. No boyfriends, no husbands, no children. Their escape from traditional roles is the core of their radicalism. It made them scary in their time and makes them thrilling in ours.

May 4, 2017. On the GOP healthcare bill and preexisting conditions: The technologies and supplies that sustain Richard's life are mainly paid for by the health plan at the university where he teaches. Richard's body produces no insulin. Were he to leave the university, it might require all of his money and mine to keep him in supplies and maintain the insulin pump and sensor he attaches to his body. In Richard's case, if you get insulin, you live. If you don't get insulin, you die. There is no middle ground. That is the nature of Type 1 Diabetes, an autoimmune disease that for multiple and incalculable reasons destroys the beta cells in the pancreas that produce insulin. This is one story among thousands and perhaps millions of chronic and incurable illnesses that preexist, just as the potential for all human beings to die preexists.

May 7, 2017. I am alone in Arizona, where I am seldom alone. Time feels larger here, like a vast desert filled with dusty vegetation. I am pretending I am a mayfly, and this day is my entire life. The hours seem large and solid, like those boulders here that are always in motion imperceptible to human senses and take 10,000 years to move from point A to point B. The evening seems an age away. I am reading several books at the same time and picking up items I want to pack, even though I can't pack the light conditions and the pinkness of the air you see only in Arizona.

May 25, 2017. I am traveling to Iceland next week, and my passport has expired. I went to Duane Reade for photos and said to a young woman, "I look sad. Can you do anything?" She said, "I'll take pictures until you look happy."

July 22, 2017. My sister died yesterday. She was nearly six when I was born. She would drink my bottles, and I would cry for food. She said, "I can only be my real self with you." I said, "Keep talking. You're still fully alive." She said, "Except I can't move." She asked me not to leave her, and I did not leave her. I fed her, cleaned her, gave her medications. The other day at a yard sale I bought a small metal box with a flower design on the lid. Inside, in a small plastic bag, were the unopened cremains of a dog or a cat. At camp after it rained, orange salamanders would appear in the little moat that formed around the tennis courts. Early mornings, I would break away from my group and run to my sister at the flagpole.

September 8, 2017. People get Darwin wrong. It's not the ruthless that survive. It's the ones that adapt.

September 10, 2017. The *Village Voice* reunion was massively touching. At one point, as the names of the dead were read in memorium, the assembled cheered, applauded, murmured softly, or fell silent. It created a weird, post mortem popularity contest, and I felt a bolt of junior-high, pit-of-the-stomach anxiety that was part of the fun.

September 18, 2017. It's Emmy time, and I'm thinking about *Fargo* and *The Americans,* two brilliantly quirky shows I love. Season 3 of *Fargo* was beautiful and funny and painful. David Thewlis plays the Devil as a bulimic in a desperate, meaningless, headlong feeding frenzy. Both shows are about the despair of imperialism discovering its emptiness. *The Handmaid's Tale,* on the other hand, is a show I hate-watch for the female-suffering porn. Its Emmy win is meant to boost feminism in that hazy, misdirected victim-as-hero association that retards women's freedom.

September 19, 2017. Every day is the break-up museum.

September 27, 2017. I am remembering Kate Millett and Lila Karp, two women who were older and gave me books to read: Violette Leduc, Jean Rhys, Doris Lessing, Colette, de Beauvoir. Lila used to cook a dish with chicken, potatoes, lemon, and butter. She was beautiful and plump, and I was interested in her freedom to use butter. Kate and Lila made rough surroundings look elegant. They knew the right arrangement of things, and I could not tell the difference between love and envy.

October 6, 2017. The plaque outside Canada's new National Holocaust Monument in Ottawa failed to mention Jews or anti-Semitism. According to the official explanation, this "appears to have been an oversight."

October 7, 2017. At a dinner party last night, I said to the man across from me, "All the judges of the Supreme Court will be women for the next 200 years, and most will be women of color. Men will stop saying things for 100 years. They will lie back on beds with their skin glowing and look beautiful. Beautiful and silent. They will adopt rescue animals and become good at listening." The man's large head moved back, and he smiled uncertainly, practiced at meeting aggression in this way. Every new language sounds harsh at first.

October 14, 2017. In Season 2 of *Better Things*, the recent episode "Phil," directed by Pamela Adlon and performed by Celia Imrie, is a giant writing accomplishment by Louis C.K. We see a woman coming unraveled, a woman dependent on a daughter whose difference from her is a continual admonishment. We see the shame in her eyes for not being brave enough for life and at the same time the exhaustion of having to admit it to herself. Adlon as her daughter is amused, pained, horny, numb, in love, and craving solitude that terrifies her as much as it does her mother.

October 16, 2017. People are writing about men changing their minds about sexism and sexual violence as women's testimonies come forward. The testimonies enlarge the public conversation about how women live, but I don't think that's how people change their minds. The only times I have changed were when I could not bear another second of myself in a certain way. Change is from within, and it issues from pain in my experience, not empathy or instruction.

October 17, 2017. In June 2005, I was leaving the Flux Factory, where I had spent a month living in a tiny house in an art gallery. I was wondering what to do next as I walked to the 7 train. There was an email from Linda Miller, asking if I would like to teach a course at Muhlenberg College, and I said, "Yes, yes I would like to teach a course." It was one of those classes where people fall in love with each other and stay in love with the memory of the gatherings.

Tonight I am at Muhlenberg College again, having dinner with Linda, who looks beautiful. Her hair is a daring color red. Tomorrow is my birthday, and I will spend it with writing students, and I could not be happier. I shared the Flux Factory gallery with the writers Ranbir Sidhu and Grant Bailie. We and the resident Fluxie artists formed a sort of circus family. Tonight I had lobster. In the past here, I would drink with Alec Marsh in a dive bar near the campus. I took a bath and missed my sister.

October 20, 2017. A male writer posted about acts he was questioning, including: asking people for a drink, flirting, and consensual affairs. Having drinks, flirting, and fucking people who want to fuck each other do not belong in the category of possible harassment! What is wrong with you people! No female has ever been confused about *I want this* and *I don't want this and you are not listening to me.* If men and boys are confused about this, it's because you want to stay confused, and I don't have time to care why. It's your job to figure out the difference and stop describing people who don't want to be slimed and brutalized as people who are leery of sex.

October 21, 2017. There is something magnetic about the situations that produce remorse.

October 26, 2017. Note to self: Don't eat something just because you cooked it.

November 2, 2017. A memory of catering from a notebook of 2001: I am assigned the raw bar along with a specialist in fish. Our station consists of large beds of shaved ice and a four-foot high ice sculpture containing an embedded publicity photo of The Duprees and two of their hit 45s. The ice sculpture begins to melt in the sun, and soon little fissures obscure The Duprees. A hose behind the table siphons run-off water into a tub.

The fish specialist is from Acapulco and has a broad, handsome face that looks like an Easter Island statue. His arm feels like the trunk of a tree. He's wearing a chef's jacket and checked pants, and his dark hair rises up from his forehead. Usually he works at the fish market on 13th Street, near the West Side Highway, starting at 4 am.

Beside our table is a metal proofer layered with dry ice and sheet pans of seafood and sauces. We cover the proofer with a white cloth to make a work surface on which we place a cutting board, knives, shuckers, and towels for opening shellfish. As we talk, the fish specialist opens oysters and clams and scrapes them to make them easy to eat. There are three types of oysters: Malpecque, Belon, and Blue Point, also Little Neck clams, plus cooked crab claws and jumbo shrimp. We set the seafood on the ice, as well as wedges of lemon and three kinds of sauces in bowls with serving spoons. I stack small plates and arrange seafood forks in a napkin nest.

The guests have deep tans. A few ask about the different oysters. Some look at the crab claws and wonder what they are. Some prepare neat plates, spooning a different sauce on each item. Most pile ten or twelve enormous shrimp onto a plate and ladle on half a bowl of sauce.

November 2, 2017. Yesterday in *The Hollywood Reporter,* Anna Graham Hunter recalled her time as a seventeen-year-old set assistant on a movie starring Dustin Hoffman: "One morning I went to his dressing room to take his breakfast order; he looked at me and grinned, taking his time. Then he said, 'I'll have a hard-boiled egg . . . and a soft-boiled clitoris.' His entourage burst out laughing."

November 5, 2017. Notes written in 2005 for an interview I conducted with Kate Millett about Norman Mailer for a French TV documentary. Always brilliant, Millett calls Mailer's yoking of macho violence to hipness "domesticated Nietzsche." Here are some other things we talked about.

MILLETT Mailer represents killing as sexual and sexuality as murderous. . . . Rape becomes something to accept as "part of life" and to be assessed on whether the act possesses "artistry" or "real desire."

LAURIE Mailer is fearful of women's arousal just like every other social and sexual conservative, and so, for women in his world, any path to eros is a subversive activity.

MILLETT Mailer doesn't want to see women freed of guilt. He becomes an archconservative, an avowed male chauvinist and propagandist against sexual liberation for women, advocating against birth control, abortion rights, and reproductive freedom.

LAURIE Mailer is basically a puritan. He likes to keep the disgust and guilt in sex, which he sees as dirty and wretched, in addition to violent. In "The Time of Her Time," about a Jewish woman's first orgasm, courtesy of Sergius O'Shaughnessy, Mailer sees "a female laid" as a female subjugated. Mailer discovers that he's never cruel enough to be a real man by his fantasy standards, so he is pussified by his own fantasies of super virility. In *Armies of the Night*, he writes "nobody was born a man," meaning, to him, a male has to become a man by subduing his homosexual side, that is, the secret woman that men contain. He does this by vanquishing actual women.

MILLETT Mailer rails against the "feminization of America," the most terrifying symptom of which to him is the "rise of homosexuality." For Mailer the violence in sex

> issues from a suppressed fear of homosexuality, which he considered a greater evil than murder.

From *Sexual Politics*, Millett's summation of Mailer's cult of machismo: "[D]riven by its values and convictions, its dualist opposition between God and the devil, male and female, virility and effeminacy, confronted by the twin perils of waning masculine dominion and the dangerous fascination of homosexuality, Mailer's 'better to murder than to burn' has brought the counterrevolutionary sensibility to a breaking point of belligerent anxiety (and perhaps we experience it in other areas too as the practice of virility grows more and more at odds with life on the planet). Machismo stands at bay, cornered by the threat of a second sexual revolution, which, in obliterating the fear of homosexuality, could challenge the entire temperamental categories (masculine and feminine) of patriarchal culture—this is where Genet is relevant."

November 17, 2017. In Alan Benson's 1984 documentary about Kathy Acker, she reads her work with quiet pleasure and a New Yawk accent that sounds like your aunt in a mink at Schrafft's. A gold tooth gives her a gap-toothed wacky grin. Her hair is a white buzz cut like a topiary. "If Janie doesn't get who she wants, she naturally revolts... Intense sexual desire is the greatest thing in the world."

November 21, 2017. I remember times when I was too flustered or worried about turning a situation awkward to say, "Take your hand off me," or "I don't like the way that feels." I wasn't young. My whole life I have not known how to behave. Masses of females now believe they will produce social change and not have to forfeit their well-being in isolation if they itemize out loud the touching, and sneering, and license taken to stop you in your tracks and say, "Smile," say, "Pay attention to me."

November 27, 2017. The other day (November 25) the *New York Times* ran a piece called "The Unexamined Brutality of the Male

Libido," by Stephen Marche, reporting as if the essential brutality of the male libido were a thing that exists. The myth of the "brutal male libido" is tenderly preserved in the paper of record like the remains of a small, endangered animal everyone loves. About the harm I have caused with my sexual behavior: No one has ever said, "That's how women are."

November 29, 2017. Number of times I've said, "I'm sorry." Number of times I've felt sorry. Number of times I've made people feel angry and uncomfortable at dinner parties for expressing my views about women. Number of times I've been called "strident" and "aggressive." Number of times a male person using my tone and language would be termed "strident" and "aggressive" to his face. Number of times I have thought my life was defined by anger. Number of times I have thought I should become softer, kinder, more open to contrasting views. Number of times I really thought this. Number of times friends have recommended Buddhism and meditation to me. Number of times I have thought no one can live an easy life with so much dissent and refusal in them. Number of times I have wondered if I would wind up entirely alone. Number of times I wondered if my outlook would destroy my writing. Number of times I have thought it was funny being stuck in my temperament and also in a world fighting hard against my desire for change. Number of times I have wondered if some people have more love in them. Number of times I have rewritten conversations in my head all night. Number of times I have felt it does not matter if your views are popular as long as they are yours. Number of times I have wanted to be loved with all my shit. Number of times I have had dreams about this.

November 29, 2017. It was chilly this morning, and I wore a black jacket with a paperclip for a zipper pull. The grass was the green of electricity, and the trees were heavy with grapefruits and lemons. It was silent. Ducks and geese paddled in the shape of a wedge. It reminded me of pie, and I missed my sister.

November 30, 2017. In response to charges of sexual harassment, playwright Israel Horovitz writes, "I apologize with all my heart to any woman who has ever felt compromised by my actions." No one feels raped. No one feels groped and forcefully kissed. Apologizers: Lose the conditional tense. You did it. Admit it. Disappear.

December 1, 2017. I am re-reading *I Love Dick* with more joy than even the first time I read it when it was published in 1997. Chris Kraus writes, "Once you've accepted total obscurity, you might as well do what you want." Yes! And there is the added benefit that the presence of the absence fuels your imagination, in that desire fulfilled is desire destroyed. According to Kraus's narrator, it doesn't matter that the person you are writing to isn't listening to you and isn't as smart as you want to believe they are. The activity of desiring turns you on so much, you write with more insight about the social world, and more detail about the physical world, and more drama about your emotional life, and more humor about the play of language than you ever believed possible.

I Love Dick is *Fatal Attraction* as told by a woman instead of a man. In the man's telling, the desiring female is a predatory menace. In the woman's telling, there is no cooked bunny and no family harmed. The male sexual predator thinks it's okay to take what he wants because he believes things are his. The female sexual predator performs a social transgression by daring to take anything. She crosses a room to stand before the object of her desire, looking him or her or some kind of liquid other in the eye and smiling in a way they cannot mistake for anything but attraction. She asks, "How about it?"

December 10, 2017. During the invasion of Afghanistan, Laura Bush tried to drum up support by proclaiming the Taliban weren't nice to women. The purpose of the war was not to rethink gender imbalance in the East or West. The atrocities meted out to women within Islamic fundamentalist regimes were well-known and documented before the Bushes declared war in the region.

Still, devious motives notwithstanding, it's a good thing that attention was paid to the deadly misogyny in Afghan culture. Should that same attention have been directed at all religions and sexist societies? Yes. Did it happen? No. Instead, the press and opponents of feminism and lots of women who considered themselves feminists focused their attention on how feminism was easily co-opted (because co-optable) by the Bush administration and the oil-hungry corporations financing the government.

It surely would have been possible to name the cynicism in Laura Bush's ploy and also seize the opportunity, as some women did in this period, to go head-to-head with the Taliban, who were and are still authorizing mutilation, murder, rape, and the forced marriage of girls and women. That the emphasis was on the co-optation of feminism and not on the insights and activism of feminists is how sexism works. Always make something more important than the insights feminists bring to gender inequality, and always find ways to tar feminism as a movement because the world-transforming program it advances is too costly to the status quo.

Now, with regard to the #MeToo movement, the press advances victim-y, girly forms of feminism because they conform to the girl gender assignment. The work remains, as it always has, to keep sex sexy, to oppose violence in all its forms and name its gendered component, to remake the world so female humans and male humans are happier, freer, and not fighting all the time for the right to food, health care, housing, and sovereignty over what their bodies wear and how they can move without threat in public space.

December 25, 2017. I asked Santa to kill HIM.

January 16, 2018. Regarding the accusations made against Aziz Ansari: The woman who reported going on a date with the actor appears to have been entirely instrumental to his wish to get off. This is a guy to ditch as soon as possible. So why, after she came out of the bathroom in his apartment and told him to chill about having sex, did she go down on him when he pulled out his penis and pointed to it? A woman who has been treated shabbily on a date and could have left skews the #MeToo wave of disclosures away from coercion, threat, aggression, and constraint to something else. How to turn male humans into better lovers and not assholes on dates? If that is the category, let's talk about that.

January 17, 2018. Some historical perspective on the pushback against #MeToo by Daphne Merkin and Katie Roiphe: There is a tradition of girls being paid by boys to beat up the other girls. It was a role Elizabeth Hardwick played before and during the second wave of feminism in such books as *Seduction and Betrayal* (1974), which reads like a guide to why women can't measure up to men. Hannah Arendt and Mary McCarthy traded letters deriding the women's movement. Diana Trilling was not a happy girl amid the social uprisings of the '60s and '70s. Partly these women wanted to maintain the status of glittering exception rather than run in a pack. Partly they did not want to identify with a group that lacked power. As individuals and exceptions, they had power—the power of borrowed light in the proximity of men.

January 21, 2018. Headline for a piece in *The Atlantic* about Aziz Ansari: "Women are Angry, Temporarily Powerful—and Very, Very Dangerous." Men should probably begin walking in pairs.

January 22, 2018. On the Louise Bourgeois show at The Museum of Modern Art: There was Bourgeois' crazy giant spider, weaving her world out of her body. There were architectural renderings of her emotional states, among them thin wood towers representing friends she missed and had left behind in France. The fabric collages were made from clothes she had worn, each a small memory palace of the life lived in those clothes. "Art is a guarantee of sanity," she said in an interview, and a moment later, "If you are an artist, you are already cuckoo." For ten years, her father had installed his mistress in the house to live with the family. Her father had been hard on her. She said she made trauma visible in order to know it and move on. She said, "I transform hate into love. That's what makes me tick."

January 23, 2018. In the Season 2 opener of *High Maintenance,* the population awakes to news of a catastrophe so pervasive and implacable it has no name. Bars and dope dealers rake in money, but money has no meaning in a world robbed of beauty and hope.

January 25, 2018. From a notebook entry written in November 1992, when I worked as a volunteer at God's Love We Deliver, the organization that fed homebound people with AIDS: last Thursday I went out with one of the vans instead of going to the kitchen. Vince, the driver, and I made deliveries to the distribution centers and a number of individual clients. The route was Queens, Brooklyn, and lower Manhattan. Clients drift in and out of the service. Mostly out, because they die. Vince told me how upset he becomes when a client doesn't respond to his ring and it turns out the person has gone to the hospital or died. Vince is small and compact. At 37, he looks younger. His sister died of AIDS last month at the age of 30. She had had unprotected sex and did not know she was infected when she married and had a child. The little girl is four. Both her husband and daughter are negative.

January 25, 2018. From a notebook entry in 1992: My mother is walking down Broadway on a windy day when suddenly something flies up and lodges between her legs. She looks down to see a head. No, it's an enormous, red wig that flows back in thick waves. A moment later a woman appears and takes the wig from my mother, saying "Thank you, thank you." My mother says to me, "She had a tape across her scalp and only a few wisps of hair." I say, "Don't laugh. Soon it will be me." But we do laugh.

February 1, 2018. A thought about data mining and genetic engineering in *The Terrible Gift: The Brave New World of Genetic Medicine,* by Rick J. Carlson and Gary Stimeling: "In twenty years, it was likely that meat would be grown in vats using genes engineered to trigger a 'buy' response in the people who ate it when they were exposed to subliminal images in commercials. Of course, the commercials wouldn't be framed as such but would be everywhere, imbedded in the image-surround. Maybe advertisers would deliver messages digitalized in proteins dissolved in mouthwash, all of which it would be impossible to spit out."

February 1, 2018. Seeing history as a downward spiral—a decline and fall, the loss of an imagined golden age that never was—is a form of castration anxiety.

February 3, 2018. Richard and I are considering buying a house together in the not-too distant future, and the first words out of his mouth are, "What if you peg it?"

February 3, 2018. A thought about complicity in times like ours, from Louis Menand's review of *Postwar: A History of Europe since 1945*, by Tony Judt, ("From the Ashes," *The New Yorker*, 28 November 2005): "The bewildering collapse of the great French Army, which folded within six weeks of the German advance in the spring of 1940; the alacrity with which many countries adapted to occupation; and the willingness to ignore, and sometimes to assist in, the deportations all made distasteful memories. Judt notes that France, a country with a population of some 40 million, was administered by 1500 Nazis, plus 6000 German policemen. A skeleton team sufficed in The Netherlands as well. Soon after Germany was defeated, a Myth of Resistance sprang up in the formerly occupied countries of Western Europe, and for many years it successfully obscured the truth about wartime life. In Austria (a country that supplied half of all concentration-camp guards), and even in Germany, people managed to convince themselves that they, too, had been Hitler's victims. In a poll conducted in 1951, only five per cent of West Germans said that they felt guilty about what had happened to the Jews; 21 per cent thought that the Jews were 'partly responsible' for their fate."

February 4, 2018. From a notebook entry about power in publishing, written on June 2, 1991: X is 34. His roommate Y is about to have his first novel published by Knopf. All of them, including Z, have been students of Gordon Lish, who is Y's editor at Knopf. Z says he thinks Lish is a negative force in these people's lives. His students all adopt certain mannerisms and repetitions like, "My mother said, 'Bill, Bill, come here. Come here. Bill', my mother said." That sort of thing. "All over the country there is a generation of young writers who use repetition because Lish's mother spoke to him in that way."

February 5, 2018. Weight lifting, tattoos, piercings, scarification, Nautilus-machine workouts, top surgery, the use of Botox and fillers, clothing, makeup, hair color, cosmetic surgery, reconstructive facial trauma surgery, breast reduction, breast augmentation, penile pumps, high heels, chest binding, the wearing of a strap-on, the wearing of a prosthetic limb, the use of an implanted pump to deliver insulin. People want to modify their bodies because it excites them, because they feel more beautiful, because they are happier living as females, or males, or liquids, or ambiguously gendered humans. Humans are technological animals with brains that transform their environments that in turn change them. Essentialism is manifest destiny under the guise of fake science.

February 5, 2018. On the pleasure of longing from a notebook entry written in April, 1993: R still harbors a passion for her former boyfriend. While we are eating, she sees a man walk past the window she thinks is him. Her former boyfriend did not think she was worthy of him, and R cannot shed the desire for him. The man who passed by the window stands in front of the restaurant and smokes a cigarette. I have seen him kissing a waitress and know he cannot be R's former boyfriend. She knows this, too, but she keeps lingering on the resemblance. She wants to be reminded that her life lacks romance.

February 7, 2018. The phrase *man hating* is an expression of woman hating.

February 8, 2018. Thank you, Tony Hoagland, for the story of my life.

"Epistle of Momentary Generosity"

I got a note from James, who used to be my friend,
In which he says he misses me,

so I hold the letter in my hand
and for a moment just appreciate

this kindness that he squeezed out of his heart
right before that muscle clenched again

and tried to make him take it back,
or add a note that says, *You dirty snake.*

You have my Leonard Cohen albums.

And thus are human beings:
not always frightened and unkind. We

have moments when the mind unclouds
and old injuries are forgiven;

when the policeman hands the criminal a cigarette
and they stand in place and smoke, and stare

out the window at the rain;
when the lifejacket is tossed

from the back deck of a ship
too big to turn around—good luck!

That freely given impulse—there it goes.
An hour later, you might regret your

open-handedness, or think it weak,
but it is gone; the blessing

can't be taken back,
and like a gull it sails

over the churning ocean,
tilting sideways for an instant

to slip between the judgment cliffs.

February 11, 2018. The publication of women's writing on sex is part of the history of human freedom. When female desire enters the public space, it lifts the lid on policed expression in general, including the public scrutiny of the male body. Once the male body is introduced for evaluation—the size of the cock, the beauty or not of other parts—nothing is protected.

February 16, 2018. Most of the smartest men I have known do not think about their privilege as men. Some deny they can have privilege because they are from poor and/or working class backgrounds. Or because they are people of color or from countries the US and the West have dominated. Some men only have to remember being children at the mercy of their mothers, and later at the mercy of women who could reject them, to recoil from fighting on the girls' team.

The smartest men I have known have not wanted to think about the effect of their privilege on the women around them and on their children. They have added their bodies to every cause for social liberation except the liberation of women. They have believed every cause came before the liberation of women, because the liberation of women implicated them. The stamp of privilege is not to see one's privilege, to think it is natural, a right, an endowment. It is not hard to understand why so many brilliant men create complex and penetrating works of art and also say fatuous and ignorant things about feminism and the women's movement. It is not hard to understand, and quit it.

POSTCARDS FROM DC

I am standing beside a small male cop. It's four days before the Kavanaugh vote, and we still have a kind of hope or momentum from the encounter with Senator Flake that went viral. I look into the eyes of the small cop and say, "You like that we're here. Admit it." I am part of a pack of bird-dogs, putting politicians on the spot. We wear purple stickers that say "Believe Survivors," so you know who we are, except you would know anyway from the fact we are standing around instead of rushing along blindly. You would know from our hectic hair and fired-up faces. The cop breaks into a smile and says he misses New Hampshire, where he's from. He's working extra shifts because we are swarming the Senate office buildings.

To our left is a tramway only Senate employees can use. Suits and uniforms disappear past the automated doors or shoot out from them on their way somewhere or nowhere. We are waiting for a senator to emerge from an elevator, flanked by guards and an entourage of hangers-on. We are waiting to rain down words on this person and pierce the insulating bubble that allows him or her to sleep at night. It's exciting to disrupt. It's tedious waiting for a mark to swim by. I take a selfie with the cop. I would show it to you, but the skin on my cleavage looks crepey.

A woman appears with red hair that waves down her cheeks. She says, "Dick Durbin is upstairs. I'm going to ask him to use the word *fascist* to describe the government." She whips around a corner, and I call out, "I'm coming with you." Her mouth is red. Her breasts swell over the neckline of her party dress. In the elevator, she knows which buttons to press to get from point A to point B. This is my first day. Earlier I trotted beside Orrin Hatch, who glided along a hall, his face under an inch of mortuary concealer, his eyes dead, looking at no one. By tomorrow I will know which buttons to press in elevators. I will have studied the faces of the senators, and it will not help much. Close up, regardless of party, most of them look like gray-thatched lumps of play dough. There are female versions, too, who wear a ruffle of terror on the edge of their blankness.

The woman with red hair leads me to the balcony of the rotunda, her kitten heels clip-clopping on the marble floors. She has been bird-dogging for three months, sleeping on couches and eating meals contributed by donors and sent to the atrium where we congregate. "There's no place else I belong in this life," she says. The balcony is surrounded by news crews, adjusting lights and lounging in the practiced rhythm of hurry-up-and-wait. The woman with red hair has made friends with a cameraman, who texts her whenever a senator is scheduled to appear. We lean against a marble column, and there is time to take in the beauty of the space with its giant windows and the gently sloping, leafy vistas beyond them. This is a public building and part of the pleasure of the moment is occupying it as if it belongs to us, flowing into the sight lines of those who govern and those who protect the people who govern. In contact zones, everything gets rubbed.

Durbin is a Democrat from Illinois. He looks like he's melting under the lights. When he finishes speaking, we corner him. The panic that washes over him has more the look of *Why the fuck are women bothering me?* than of a man on the wrong side of the vote. The woman with red hair says, "We are living under fascism. Will you use this word in your statements?" His eyes shift down as he says, "I like to be exact in my words." I look at him, and he meets my eyes. I say, "I think everyone believes what the women are saying. They just don't care. Is that about right?" He gives me a nervous nod and says, "That's a possibility."

This is the spiel I will deliver for two days to senators on both sides. We are instructed to cheer those opposing Kavanaugh and to confront the people on his side as well as those in the weasel category "undecided," as if Flake, Collins, Manchin, et. al, have been scripted by a Magic 8-Ball to say, "Answer hazy, ask again later." I will see Cruz, who has the painted-on hair of a ventriloquist's dummy, surrounded by what look like armed guards. I will not see Flake, who is in hiding, as is Collins. I will go to Flake's office with a posse, and we will write personal notes to him. I will catch sightings of Amy Klobuchar and Mazie Hirono and shout cheers. I will waylay Cory Booker long enough to say, "I so fucking appreciate what you're doing," and he will flash one of his neon smiles and say, "That means a lot to know."

The cops make friends with us, even if they don't want to. The news crews too. They're cued to what's happening before we are, and we hop on their stakeouts like yellow-billed oxpeckers feeding on the backs of zebras. It reminds me of the month I spent in Alaska in 1989 covering the Exxon oil spill, and the way disasters create their own cultures with surprising affinities. One day a man I will call a disaster entrepreneur—he had a contract from the Alyeska Pipeline Service Company to clean up a stretch of oiled beach—took me out with him. We drove dune buggies with giant rubber tires along the rocky coast, and the wind took us, and afterward we went for drinks and spoke of the natural world we both cared about. Kavanaugh is a disaster everyone feels here. You can see pain in people's faces, and little threat is directed our way by the cops. Most people in disasters are kinder, weirder, freer—except for those responsible for the disaster, and sometimes me.

I speak with a woman a generation younger who has a stunning, asymmetrical haircut and glowing lips. She has been organizing in South Carolina and has swerved her car to come to DC for the same reason we all have: because we could not do otherwise. This work is what she does all the time. She uses the terms *social justice* and *intersectional* but does not once say *feminist, feminism,* or *women's movement.* When I use these words, her mouth turns down, as if her orgasms might be at risk in proximity to such unsexy language, as if white privilege and unconscious racism have wafted in on the backs of these terms.

In other conversations, I try (and fail) to keep my mouth shut about the word *survivor,* stamped on t-shirts and signs. It's meant to signal virtue, which to me is reason enough to kill it. I don't think we survive anything. I think trauma and sadness have natural histories inside everyone. Then I shut up about trauma. I've gone to a rally outside the Supreme Court. Kirsten Gillibrand has eloquently emphasized Kavanaugh's positions on abortion rights and executive privilege, as well as his emotional unfitness for the bench, instead of focusing on his sexual loathsomeness. Her clarity alternates with a churchy vibe. People say *sacred* and *holy* to cheers. A female rabbi speaks, and then another woman says a prayer in Hebrew, and I'm up to here with the way piety and good-girl-itis attach themselves to women's causes. In Alaska, oiled beaches and dead animals notwithstanding, at least no one prayed.

I step out of the mass of people and take a seat on a curb beside a row of shrubs where I talk to a trans person I've met while bird-dogging. The person is tall and wearing women's clothes. I never catch the person's pronouns, so I will use "they." They say they have slipped away from the rally because they have been "triggered" by a story of sexual abuse someone has told. The word *trigger,* so overused, has become associated with cordoning off excitement, and when I hear it I feel like a rat getting shocked while reaching for a food pellet. They explain they were tied to a chair and left in a shack believing they would die, and as I listen I tell myself to shut up and dial down my own signal reactions.

The second day at the Senate offices, dozens more people arrive, including many men. A contingent has flown in from Seattle. We are every color, age, and apparent gender. A man who looks South Asian is so well dressed I approach him and say, "Are you a ringer?" He laughs and tells me about his day job as a longtime activist, working for progressive causes in and out of government. I bird-dog with a crew that includes a male reporter for *The Nation,* who has come from Oakland, a woman from Boston who was arrested twice the week before in civil disobedience actions, and several other women who live near the Capitol and bird-dog often. We run into the same cops, who by now are telling us stories about their lives. A slender female cop teasingly blames us for being here so much she can't adopt a dog. We patrol the halls like delinquents cutting class and I run into the woman with red hair. She needs to figure out where she will sleep that night. It turns out we live close to each other in New York. She says, "I will stalk you." I say, "I bet you say that to all the girls."

Wednesday night I head back to New York by train. I am writing this Saturday. Kavanaugh has been confirmed. I feel less *something,* having gone. What's the word? *Passive*? *Done to*? A little while ago I told a friend I thought we should bird-dog until this government is unseated. Two thousand of us there every day, taking turns, everyone in the country taking a shift, subsidized for those who need it. She said, "What good will it do?" I said, "They don't expect us to be there. They are used to privacy, and there we were." I thought about those giant white buildings, humming with power like an engine turning over. You have to put your belongings on a scanner to get in, but you can get in. All the people in those buildings moving along, their faces aloof, trying to ignore us, unable to ignore us. All those people believing the buildings are theirs as they look down, making deals about our lives, and there we were, rushing the walls of the panopticon, moment after moment, in tunnels and elevators and hallways. We reversed the gaze, and it felt like the opposite of despair.

THE CLOCK

October 13, 2018. I love the man who injects my face with Botox and fillers. His face glows from something he puts on his skin. I say, "I hate the pouchy thing under my right eye." He looks at it for half a second in the bright light of his office and says, "There's nothing I can do about it at this point." I say, "I hate it." He says, "The things I could do would make it worse." I say, "Okay," and he does stuff to the lines that could become puppet lines, and they disappear, and I go off into the world with my pouchy eye, not really okay that things can't all be fixed but full of love for this man who does not lie to me.

BODY LANGUAGE

Last night I watched *My Dinner with Hervé,* an HBO movie about the French actor Hervé Villechaize, who played Tattoo on *Fantasy Island* and gained fame and wealth in the 1970s and '80s. He was a dwarf, and in the film is portrayed by Peter Dinklage, wearing black wigs and speaking in a high-pitched French accent so full of grief and mischief he conjures the sadness of everyone ensnared by biology. Those half-lowered eyes. That smile of pain and knowledge. The movie is a bit corny. Jamie Dornan, who plays a journalist sent by a UK newspaper to write a lampoon of Villechaize, is outplayed in scenes by Dinklage because Dornan's role is to be guided and to discover a sense of identification.

Today I flew over mountains that were right there, dark shadows rippling over bright brown rock. The lift-off felt like the breath-catch of sex, and I wondered if I could fall in love with the body of a stranger. I was thinking about the threat made last week by the Trump administration to define out of existence the concept of transgender and how this thinking is also a threat to female humans, whether or not they acknowledge it. Females, homosexuals, trans people, gender-fluid people, people who defy gendered dress codes and body norms, all undermine the notion of maleness as a one-stop, biologically-determined thing owed supremacy. If maleness were an essential thing, nothing could weaken its dominance. It would exist inviolate, like an atom of oxygen in a molecule of water. Everyone on the planet knows you have to protect maleness all the time or the truth of people's hybrid nature will force a redistribution of power between the sexes. That would cost a lot of money.

I am on your street. I remember a parquet square that had crumbled like a cracker under a planter. I don't look up in case you are at the window or someone else drifts by with a scarf at her neck. When I first saw the floors of your apartment, I thought of an animal one rescues from the street. You had a leather couch with metal studs along the edges, like a dentist's couch, ugly and hard. I want to ask you something when I pass your building. I think of what I would say if we bumped into each other and went for coffee like friends who cannot remember why they drifted apart. The other night I killed two moths that had flown through the window to the small lamp beside my bed. I was careful to kill them without leaving powder on the rug or walls. They had more life in them than I was comfortable ending. Outside, grass poked up through the paving stones and purple light reflected off the river.

The other week I saw *On Beckett*, a solo piece by the actor and clown Bill Irwin. It was moving and tender because Irwin has devoted himself to Beckett's rueful, mordant monologues, cemented in physical detail. It is the love of a son for a broken-down father who had once been the world. With Beckett, you are more inside a mind that is on all the time than inside a being with a sex. Before the lights dimmed, I wondered if Beckett would pass the *Breaking Bad* Test. The *Breaking Bad* Test is when you are helplessly swept into a show with male characters who have dimension and say surprising things while the female characters do not pass the Bechdel Test. The Bechdel Test is when two female characters talk to each other about something other than men. The *Breaking Bad* Test is a variant of the *Moby Dick* Test, where only male humans are real to the creator or only male characters exist, and yet if you are not male, not whale, not doing meth, or not inclined to hunt marine mammals, you do not notice your absence in a way that causes you to leave the theater or kick the book in the head. You enter a love letter to attraction that folds itself around you like your own dream. You remember a cat that blurred the outline of your body. Also a bird.

The deeper the awareness that male supremacy isn't produced by nature, the higher the degree of panic. The higher the degree of panic, the more brutal the enforcement of gender separation and the quarantining of bodies, lest maleness itself be contaminated and fatally weakened by proximity to femaleness and other nonbinary bodies. The panic suggests to those fighting the hardest that the contamination has already set in. The attack on othered bodies is a denial of knowledge that really can't be erased.

When I read stories set in a French villa or an Italian villa, where meals are eaten on patios and lawns under striped awnings, where there are always three courses served on gleaming china, vegetables from a nearby farm, eggs from local chickens, charcuterie sliced paper thin, cutlets sautéed with capers and butter sauce on the side, glasses of wine and bubbly water, mild breezes cooling summer days, a family and their guests or the young inheritors of wealth with a houseful of sexy, happy, bored, and terrified people, all I can think about are the servers doing the work.

My Dinner with Hervé takes place in 1993 when Hervé is out of money and hope. The woman he married has left him and broken something that can't be repaired. He wonders if he actually loved her or only wanted to prove he could be loved. All his life he has been made to feel less than whole because of his size. As the costar of *Fantasy Island,* he sought to earn as much money as Ricardo Montalbán, a demand thought absurd to everyone but him. The night following his meeting with the journalist, he shoots himself in the head.

Everything stops too soon when you are expecting the next note. When I imagine rebooting a lost relationship, I am reminded of a passage from Beckett's novel *Murphy*: "A man is in bed, wanting to sleep. A rat is behind the wall at his head, wanting to move. The man hears the rat fidget and cannot sleep, the rat hears the man fidget and dares not move." Every time I have told myself to accept the limits of another person, I have gone nuts like the previous time.

A few times I stayed in bed with you, knowing a writer or a musician was waiting to talk to me in a café. It was a time before cell phones, and the writer or musician would be sitting there, checking the clock. After you left, I took to watching a cooking show with a chef who wore his hair long like yours and had your dark skin and sad smile. If I ran into you, I would not ask you the question. I would say, "Have you repaired the parquet square?" I remember when I was younger and in pain from love. I would walk for whole days and nights, day after day and night after night as if I had all the time in the world to let time do what time can do. I do not have that kind of time anymore, but maybe I would still walk, not knowing what else to do.

In 1966, I married a man and moved into a bourgeois high-rise in the West Village. Next door to us lived Adele Morales, who had been married to Norman Mailer and had been stabbed by him an inch or so from her heart. To think of transphobia apart from gynephobia and misogyny is to miss a core structure of male supremacy. Likewise, any woman who does not see her predicament as intimately linked to the predicament of trans people and other nonconforming bodies has a sadly enfeebled understanding of the world.

Adele was raising her two daughters, and we could hear each other's lives through the thin wall we shared. We decided the hell with privacy and became friends. Everything in her life seemed glamorous to me, and she was warm and beautiful with skin the color of dusty roses. She was acting in those days and performed in several plays directed by the great Downtown actor and playwright Julie Bovasso. Hervé and Adele were both cast in a Bovasso production. He wore a Napoleon costume and barked the word *shtupping* several times as a punch line.

The play had the quality of a dream, and during its run Adele and the man I was married to and I had a party together, with people flowing into both apartments. That's the night I met you. You were working full time against the war. We would run into you at a camp site in Northern Spain the summer Nixon resigned, and we would drink all night in celebration. Hervé came to that party, too, and ate the Swedish meatballs I was preparing in those days. He was charming and seemed a little lost and also self-possessed in something of the manner Dinklage captures in his performance. That time came swimming back, as things do when your life has been touched.

THE CLOCK

February 16, 2018. I watched *Wonder Woman* last night and liked Gal Gadot, who plays her. Good bracelets, but what's with the sex? Wonder Woman's name is Diana, after the goddess of the hunt and chase, who is celibate. No penis was called upon at her conception. Zeus formed her from clay, etc. She grows up with a band of horse-riding Amazons, including her mother. She does not see a man until one drops from the sky like Icarus, and she saves his life. They fall in love but don't have sex. He dies, sacrificing himself to save a lot of people, and she thinks about him for the rest of the life we're shown. In sum: virgin birth, celibacy, and tough women don't fuck, not even each other. She saves the world from very bad people and does not get to have sex. In *Broadcast News*, Holly Hunter jumps umpteen hurdles and still does not get to have sex with William Hurt. She doesn't even get to eat. It's a thing to withhold pleasure from female characters shown to be virtuous. Punish them by making them good, and then punish them again by requiring they abstain from fun.

February 18, 2018. My sister hasn't been dead long. I wish I could see you again, smiling quizzically, your mouth twisted to the side, one eyebrow cocked. Decisions made outside you are shadows.

February 19, 2018. It rained in Scottsdale for one day and part of another. The power cut out, and the garage door couldn't open. The nearest shopping center was a few miles away. I walked along

Arabian. All the streets here are named for horses. I picked two lemons hanging over a wall. The traffic lights were out. I could see myself standing in the road at Shea Blvd. and 84th Street. I thought I would do a good job directing traffic. I watched the cars for a while, and they didn't seem to need me. I walked on.

Two cops were directing traffic at the exit off the 101 highway. They looked professional, waving at cars. I didn't think I would have done as well, and I was reminded of how often I believe I can do things I know nothing about. This thought was not depressing. It showed I was willing to fail.

I arrived at the shopping center, and the power came back on. I passed a Marshalls. I had never been inside a Marshalls and decided to enter. I needed a pair of Reef flip-flops. My ankle was sore from backing into a barrel cactus. The Reefs were sold out. A tall woman with yellow hair gave me Nike flip-flops, marked down from $35 to $13. I was excited by the markdown and twirled around like a dog on a couch. The woman was excited, too. She could have been high.

I didn't have money or credit cards. She put aside the flip-flops until I could return. This is the kind of thing that is normal is Scottsdale if you are white. Today I walked in the flip-flops around several man-made lakes and picked two grapefruits. It was windy, and the sky was overcast, like a beach day. These conditions occur here once in a blue moon.

February 20, 2018. I watched Season 4 of *Mozart in the Jungle* and cried. This morning in bed, I described to Richard what had stirred me, and cried again. During the first three seasons we saw the migration of a young woman from small town USA to NYC to pursue a career as a classical musician. She plays the oboe, and she is quickly smitten by the mercurial young genius conductor from Mexico, who takes command of what is meant to be the New York Philharmonic.

This season, the oboe player, Hailey (Lola Kirke), decides she wants to conduct as well, and she finds a means to study. She has a history of quitting in the crunch, partly because music was her father's idea before it was hers. The trajectory of the conductor,

Rodrigo, is the opposite. He chose music as an arrow into the world. As Rodrigo, Gael Garcia Bernal has enormous charisma, playing an artist abuzz with ability, good will, restlessness, and appetite.

As the season progresses, he grows increasingly lost. His struggle is personal. What Hailey has to do to become a person has a social and historic dimension. For advice, Rodrigo talks to Mozart. Hailey talks to Fanny Mendlesohn, Maria Ana Mozart (Mozart's sister), and the female devisers of Kabuki, who were not allowed to perform in their own creations. In the course of this season, we see Hailey become herself, not a version of Rodrigo.

We're shown the reason it's hard for women to become conductors. During a competition in Japan, two hide-bound male judges determine only one female can be in the final five, so another woman with talent is eliminated, and Hailey is up against four men. The show is focused on the way these revelations of unfairness and so many others work on the psyches of women. At the end of the season, the two most powerful men in Hailey's life cheer for her accomplishments, earned on her own terms. I cried because the men want her to succeed.

February 27, 2018. "So close," said the fly, buzzing against the window, "but this is not the way out."

February 28, 2018. Last night Richard and I watched *Glengarry Glen Ross*. What? Glengarry. When? Last night. And? Well. Yes? He had seen it. Before? Yes. With other people? People were present. Forgive me. That will cost you. The cast. Are you speaking about the cast? The cast was. What is your point? The actors. Quite a cast, wouldn't you say? Alec Baldwin was thin. And your point? Thin Alec played morons. You were saying? The cast was all. What? Male. Really? It was clear. You mean the rain? It was *Moby Dick* without. Yes? A marine mammal.

March 5, 2018. The effects of *High Maintenance* (HBO) are difficult to pin down, and that is part of its appeal. You feel off balance while watching. You're not sure what you're looking at and what you are being shown. Richard remarked, "The style of the show produces the feeling of being stoned." Style holds the show together as well as the central character, called "the Guy," who deals pot and edibles on his bicycle to customers in Brooklyn, where he lives. It's a soft-edged, high-hazed shaggy Brooklyn of graffiti art and sub-cultures bleeding into each other. One episode entered the world of pot-smoking orthodox Jews. The Guy (Ben Sinclair, one of the creators of the show with Katja Blichfeld), is the candyman who arrives with his metal-cornered little suitcase. My favorite aspect of the show is the way it substitutes character for plot.

Usually each episode brings us into the apartment of one of the Guy's customers. We enter the scene before he does. He's a Rosencrantz or Guildenstern, dropping into a drama-in-progress he has to piece together. *In media res* is the method of the show, and it feels like going on a long walk without a destination. In one episode a friend suggests a partnership that would involve meeting customers in a car, and the Guy declines the offer saying, "But then we wouldn't see the apartments." Sadness or melancholy or vague yearning hovers over the show. Happiness almost always requires a drug. Life without drugs is hard to bear, and this seems especially apt during the past eighteen months of Our Shared Unhappiness.

The Guy is getting on in years, nearing his late 30s, and he's still dealing pot, as he did in college. What does he want? Does he need to want something other than what he has? Is he bored by the repetition of his routines? He is wary of involvement, yet he becomes involved. He helps one customer who is agoraphobic leave his apartment. He helps a pregnant woman get a ride to the hospital. He listens to people's worries. Above all, he isn't judgy. It appears to be his temperament and his offering. He wants to stay in one piece by the end of the day, which isn't always possible. In one episode he's robbed, in another he's knocked off his bike and his arm is broken.

A recent episode centered on a teenaged girl, the daughter of a woman still dining out on her East Village sexual conquests of the

'90s. It's the daughter's birthday, and three of her female friends spend the night in her house, drinking and using drugs paid for by her mother. They dance. One girl gives another a tattoo. They smoke and one girl passes out. The camera lovingly follows the birthday girl, who often finds herself cleaning up after other people. She is sad and also yearning for something. She draws, alone in her room. Late at night she slices a large piece from her uneaten birthday cake. Later, she serves it to a blonde woman her mother's age who is visiting from a Scandinavian country. In a surreal and beautiful moment, the girl kisses the blonde woman passionately, and the woman responds. They stop shortly and go their separate ways in the house. It is a large event and a mysterious event that moves us.

March 7, 2018. Richard and I were walking along a path on a greenway and came to a wayside memorial with a few carnations and a remembrance card that's been washed out except for the word, "praying." The memorial was small and close to the ground. I said, "Who do you think it's for?" Richard said, "An animal." I said, "What kind of animal?" He said, "A praying mantis."

April 7, 2018. I was surprised to see two people in particular at the *Village Voice* reunion last September. One was a man and the other was a woman, two relationships that were no longer alive and that had shaped my life in certain ways. There they were, and there I was, in readiness. The woman was bored and had been casting around for something to distract her. The man and I bumped into each other over a bowl of pita wedges and moved to a corner. In both conversations there were moments where the other person said, "Why did you say that?" or "I didn't understand why you did that," or "I thought you were angry." In neither case was anything resolved. In neither case was there an idea of resuming, and I came away feeling happy and sad. It was like wandering in the "Garden of Earthly Delights" or in a dream of your past as a Dickens ghost. What remains is the sense of who you love, not why, not *Is it equal*?

April 14, 2018. I read the piece by Junot Díaz in *The New Yorker* (April 16, 2018), about having been raped as an eight-year-old boy. He summarizes the way the experience separated him from his childhood and sense of self, pitching him into depression and states of anger he did not begin to recover from until, many years later with a long string of failed relationships behind him, he found a therapist who helped him face what had happened. The rapes (there appear to have been two) are not described in detail. Díaz mentions having gotten erections during the experience as part of the shame he felt and possibly still carries. He mentions being penetrated as something so terrible he cannot reveal the experience except to say it happened.

The piece asks us to feel that the worst pain a male can experience is to be treated the way ordinary females are treated all the time. Perhaps the worst thing that happened to Díaz came from the culture that equates being penetrated with being ruined as a man. The moment Díaz was raped, he stopped being male, he felt. He does not say this as bluntly as I am saying it, but he does use words to that effect. Dominican males are not raped, therefore…

In the piece, there is no contemplation of the way society conflates rape-able with female-ness. Díaz just conflates them. He is telling one story about one boy. What happened to him and the ways it shaped his life are painful. Ineluctably, though, when you write a piece like this, you are also writing about all rapes everywhere, except you aren't. You are making a special category for the rape of a male as particularly dreadful because it includes "unmanning." You are saying the rapes that happen to women are less terrible because they don't include "unmanning." The rapes that happen to women more or less fit their gender assignment.

While it's important for male victims of rape to speak about their experiences, it is equally important we do not draw a line between male rape and female rape. The category is rape. Not what kind of awful it is, depending on the body it happens to.

A later thought. People commented on this post, mentioning the expectations placed on women to absorb the pain of traumatized men. I thought of Hamlet and Ophelia. Hamlet is traumatized by his father's murder at the hands of his uncle (now also married to his mother) and by his failure to kill Claudius to avenge his father's death. He takes it all out on Ophelia with cruel jabs. And what does she do? She goes mad and winds up drowning herself in a river. Hamlet continues to see himself as a victim and a girly man for not committing murder.

April 18, 2018. In a mind-expanding, beautifully written piece about *2001* (*The New Yorker*, April 23, 2018), Dan Chiasson describes how Stanley Kubrick created not only films but the taste for being able to appreciate them. How *2001* predicted the future it in fact designed in its costumes, sets, furniture, and gadgets. How it created its own precursors in both directions in the same way the film looks at human existence from the time of apes on the verge of becoming human to humans on the verge of becoming star-baby-what-the-fuck-evers. How in HAL the film imagined a psychotic computer, not unlike our current too dumb and too smart algorithms that learn to be weird on their own.

April 20, 2018. According to a *Newsweek* (April 12, 2018) report, one-third of Americans don't believe that six million Jews were murdered during the Holocaust. In some conspiracy theories, historical fact is erased: the Holocaust and the moon landing are examples. In other conspiracy theories, a wished-for event is declared true: the Jews (them again) planned the World Trade Center attacks, vaccines cause autism, and ending male supremacy increases penis size. Sometimes conspiracy theories turn up facts: Lee Harvey Oswald did not act alone, Nixon was a crook, Putin engineered the ascendancy of Trump.

April 23, 2018. What are the odds of getting shat on by two different birds in the span of two hours in New York City?

April 27, 2018. The eyebrows of Sandra Oh are set high on her face. One eyebrow says, "I feel concerned." The other eyebrow says, "I don't understand." Oh plays women enlivened by work and friendship, who are bored after romantic love is secured. In *Killing Eve,* she hunts for a psychotic, Russian-paid assassin who kills in clever ways with sharp objects and enjoys watching life drain from the eyes of her prey. In Oh's most interesting scenes on *Grey's Anatomy,* she would get into bed with her best friend, and the women would sleep together under the covers.

April 30, 2018. *Homeland* began Season 7 with a breathtaking scene of Claire Danes as Carrie beating the shit out of a cyberstalker, taking his computer, and threatening to kill him if he advanced on her again. Then the show removed her child from her custody. There was no reason for the sister to demand custody of her child. The sister could still have pitched in to care for Franny. *Homeland* ended the season with the first female president resigning as a martyr to the country's well-being and with Carrie left maddened as she, too, martyrs herself. How are the guys doing? The Russian guys are fine, the American guys are fine. One American guy is now president. None of the guys is nuts. No guy is without a job.

According to the TV series *The Handmaid's Tale,* there has never been a global women's movement. Also, the repressive gender codes of Gilead actually depict societies that exist now, not in some fantasy, dystopian future but in places like Iran and Afghanistan where Sharia, Wahhabi, and Jewish fundamentalist theocratic laws govern civil society. Somehow, this pain isn't dramatic and tragic, only the pain of Western women in a similar plight. The red robes the handmaids wear are burkas. The masks that will be introduced in later episodes are veils. The mouths of handmaids will be sewn together to ensure they can't speak.

The Handmaid's Tale and *Homeland* come at precisely the moment when, in reality, women have organized in #MeToo and other forms of mass resistance. They have been the least passive, the most vocal in reaction to the sabotage of our country. Female-suffering porn is not cautionary or prophetic. It's the comfort zone of narratives that want women the old fashioned way: virtuous and deprived, or gratified and dangerous.

May 2, 2018. I am sitting on a traffic island on Broadway and 81st Street, eating chive cream cheese with a fork and listening to "The Creatures of Prometheus" on my ear pods. A soft breeze, heading to the river, moves across my cheek. Everyone is easy in summer clothes. Before I ate the cream cheese, I ate a tub of shrimp salad and another tub of Moroccan carrot salad with slivered almonds and pomegranate seeds. An extraordinarily handsome man catches my eye. He is on the bench across from me, eating pieces of mango and watching a pigeon hop around in the pattern of a square. I do not disturb them. I cannot move.

May 2, 2018. In *The Way We Were,* Barbra Streisand longs for Robert Redford, entranced by his impenetrability. Her hair is frizzy. His hair is smooth and gold. It's 1944, and she spots her college crush at El Morocco, dazzling in a white naval officer's uniform, dead asleep on a bar stool.

The film explores love that doesn't end because it can't be fulfilled, and by centering on female desire it broke ground in 1973. The movie burrows into Katie. The iconic Redford character Hubbell is the Garbo we can't know and who can't articulate himself. Katie (and later Carrie Bradshaw on *Sex and the City*) tries to discover what's inside the aloof, shadowy man, but it's impossible because the man is unknown to himself. The woman remains in the relationship, because inside the blank of her man she finds space for the renewal of erotic fantasy.

Katie's attraction to Hubbell makes him feel alive, and he enjoys her delight in him more than he delights in her. Her belief in his talent makes him think he can be a writer, but writers need something they burn to say, and Hubbell doesn't want to speak. Redford is good at incarnating "no." In scene after scene, as he paces around, looking sideways at anything but the situation he's in, his bottled emotions peek out of his eyes like hostages in a bank robbery, before they are again corralled out of sight.

May 13, 2018. Some of my tenderest mothers have been men.

May 17, 2018. What are we doing when we post videos of private citizens without their consent? Are we citizen journalists reporting news? What kind of journalists? The tabloid kind that stake out public figures and sell their pictures to other outlets?

It's great when we record members of the police and military abusing their power. Does this category extend to the video that's gone viral about the racist white guy threatening to call ICE because workers in a restaurant were speaking Spanish? I don't care that this man's privacy was violated. The privacy of poor people is violated all the time by the social agencies that organize their lives. I care about the principle of protecting the privacy of ordinary people as they conduct their lives, a category that is huge and includes me.

I don't want to live in a society where citizens out each other publicly because they scorn a value or action. I loathe the culture of calling out and right thinking. I don't know where this video fits. It's a real question. New technologies create new social circumstances that require us to rethink moral as well as legal categories, even for a guy described in a post as "a gay Jewish Nazi lawyer." I have been criticized for opposing gendered double standards, including their expressions in all religions. Opposing religion was construed as a form of bigotry. That's the problem with letting anyone's bible determine who gets shamed and why.

May 28, 2018. I proved to Twitter I was not a robot, although I am a robot.

June 4, 2018. Yesterday was the birthday of a friend, and I joined her and another friend at the home of a third friend, who lives in a leafy part of New Jersey. Four women who go back more than 50 years with different combinations of attachment and drifty knowledge of each others' lives. High school plays and summer camp. Marriages, children, divorces, break-ups, the deaths of parents and siblings, grandchildren. We did not talk about these things or much about our work. We gave each other back rubs and sat around a table in a giant kitchen no one cooked in. Seven years ago, one of the women had received a blow on the head by a large fallen tree limb, and the rest of us had formed a band to hold her life together until she could resume it. It had taken a year. We drank wine and went out to a Japanese restaurant.

I find it hard to sleep in New York, and last night I slept for nine hours. The two women who had married became feminists after their divorces. In our twenties, the friend on whom the tree had fallen and I had been in a consciousness-raising group a little while after college. We had lived near each other in the Village. Weekends, we would bike to the Morton Street pier, stretch out on towels, and talk to strangers. She would say, "Come back to my place for dinner. I'll make salad." And there, in her fridge, would be cheeses and smoked meat she had already bought. I was there when the tree limb fell and rode with her in the ambulance. Some people are strays and some people take you in.

June 5, 2018. Piranhas eat injured piranhas. An injured piranha, while being eaten, will continue to eat its original prey although part of it has been eaten by other piranhas. Discuss.

June 8, 2018. From a notebook entry written on January 7, 1995: I say to my mother, "Sasha isn't doing so well. He's old." She says, "No, he's not." I say, "He's having trouble moving. He has arthritis. He's peeing on the floor. And he's very old." She says, "You have to exercise him. He's not old. What does the vet say?" I say, "That he's never seen a dog as old as Sasha. He doesn't get to treat 18-year-old dogs." She says, "He's inexperienced. He doesn't know what he's doing."

June 19, 2018. I'm at Apple, waiting for a genius. A woman, a man, and a child are speaking Spanish near me. The man and the child leave, and the woman explains she was telling the man about an app that lets her spy on her boyfriend to see if he is cheating. She explains how it works. I say, "But you will be a spy." Her lip rises in a crooked smile. She has an attractive, Frida-Kahlo mustache. Her body is ample, her eyebrows animated. She says, "I don't care if I'm a spy. I could get AIDS." I say, "That's a point." I say, "Do you check his phone for texts?" She says, "I have a boyfriend. He doesn't sleep over much." I say, "Have you done this before?" She nods and says, "They all cheat." She shows me the ad for the app and says, "Are you going to get it?" I say, "Not right now." She says, "You seem so interested." I say, "I'm interested in you."

June 20, 2018. Yesterday on a flight I watched *The Post,* about the publication of *The Pentagon Papers* and heroic whistle-blower Daniel Ellsberg. *The Pentagon Papers* were first published by *The Washington Post.* The movie is a bouquet of clichés, save for performances by two great TV actors: Bob Odenkirk and Matthew Rhys. I had the weirdest feeling watching it, the sensation of reverse sci-fi, as if the past, with its innocence and dawning awareness of continuous political lies, was unreal and magical, had never happened, could never have been, although I had lived through it with the amazement and excitement of the people depicted in the film.

The Pentagon Papers reported findings of a study commissioned by Robert McNamara. Why would you want to compile data on the corruption and deceit behind US involvement in the war in Vietnam, policies you promoted? Why did the Nazis meticulously record their atrocities? We now live in a fog of belief in the terrible and the hopeless. We live in Nixon's mind. Nixon was always Trump, the same inconceivably unhappy and misery-generating machine.

From the perspective of now, the release of *The Pentagon Papers,* the Watergate findings, the disclosure of massive Cold War deceit in the books of John Le Carré, swaddled in the rueful gloom of Graham Greene, all of this looks like pastoral fantasy and like a stage of young adult understanding we can never recapture. *The Pentagon Papers* revealed that 70% of US policy in Vietnam was enacted to avoid the "humiliation" of having taken the wrong turn. It was about the anxiety of not asking for directions.

In *The Post,* when Daniel Ellsberg is asked why he is risking jail, he says, "Wouldn't you be willing to go to jail to end the war in Vietnam?" Justice Black, in his 6-to-3 Supreme Court vote in favor of publishing *The Pentagon Papers,* stated the press exists to serve the governed, not the governors. In the 1970s, people believed a moral society was possible and the revelations would produce reform. The morass of our social reality now is deepened by the day and hour by Julian Assange and company, by psychographics, by fake news, by colossal amounts of money spent to keep people stupid, truly uneducated. Dumb is good. Dumb is better than greed to keep people mean. Mean enough to feel good about hurting children.

June 22, 2018. From a Facebook post today by poet Patrick Donnelly: "If you need any further insights into the characters of the people who did this, please consider: They took away the children's toys, just as they had taken away their parents' rosaries. They forbid anyone to hold or comfort the children, though now we're finding out some kids have been beaten and abused (and where are the girls?) and subjected to bizarre vaccination routines. They gave the contracts for housing—caging—the children to companies which they had invested in . . . They shipped the children all over the country, until the airlines began refusing to do so. They instituted no tracking system by which families might be united, obviously never intending that they would be reunited. They lied about what they were doing, and denied it, and blamed it on their political opponents. They said the children were actors and mocked their grief. Yesterday they said they were going to stop separating children from families, but didn't mention that instead they will put whole families together in indefinite detention. They make it impossible to apply for asylum. They made illicit border crossing a felony, previously a misdemeanor, which will allow them to separate the children from the parents once again."

June 23, 2018. The average temperature in Scottsdale these days is 112 degrees in the shade. There is no shade. When the temperature reaches 120 degrees, the airports close, and the mountains melt into the valley. The vegetation bakes to crisps, and Richard and I achieve our 10,000 steps by walking in a shopping mall. It takes 100 minutes to walk four miles past Cartier, Bulgari, Jimmy Choo,

Montblanc, Williams-Sonoma, L'Occitane, Tesla, and stores that sell only baseball caps.

We smell Cinnabons and pretzels popped from ovens. The stores blend into each other with their half-hearted seductions. How can you want me when I am bored with myself? We are happy ratties darting around our maze. It's hard to say what the mall is these days. Once it was a spiral of commerce that killed the town with its open squares, winding streets, shifting neighborhoods, and chance encounters. Now, malls, too, have been abandoned. Perhaps we've slipped beyond the temptations of the physical to those of the digital, where, once seduced, we find all our desires bound together in the small, beeping lozenge of our phones.

June 29, 2018. Some of the most defining experiences I had as an undergraduate at Barnard arose from relationships with faculty. I didn't have sex with them. There were other kinds of intimacies I think now would make those older people worry they were doing some boundary-shit thing wrong. It was a time of great love, sharing, openness, invitations into people's homes and passions, and there you stood, wanting to be filled up. Sex was with anyone you wanted to have sex with. We were protesting the war in Vietnam and inventing the women's movement. These people I looked up to taught me to think and care about the world.

July 6, 2018. The author of *The Incest Diary* had sex with her father from the time she was three until she was 21. She has published an account of this experience and chosen to remain unnamed.

Some reviewers have questioned the truth of the narrative because the text is artfully constructed with layered movements back and forth in time. Other reviewers have faulted the literary accomplishment because the author describes the sex she experienced in ways that purposely arouse the reader and arouse the writer as she recalls it. Some reviewers have discredited an account of abuse that includes the child's initiation into sexual pleasure.

The author learned about sex from her father, and sex and the many colors of pleasure remain prized by her, perhaps above all other sensation and all other forms of aliveness. "Sex is the center of things," she writes. "If you're having it, it's the center. If you're not, it's the center." For a brilliant dissection of the many queasy responses the book has prompted, read Amia Srinivasan's essay, "Silent Treatment, a Troubling Response to an Incest Memoir" (*Harper's*, March 2018).

Here are some things we learn in the book. The narrator's father entered parts of her body before they were large enough to accommodate his penis. One day her bath water turned red with blood. She learned to float above her body and look down from the ceiling or a cloud at a girl on a bed. She had orgasms that filled her with desire and loneliness. In dance class, she was afraid to open her legs, fearing people would know she'd had intercourse. She was afraid to stick out her tongue, believing people could tell she licked her father's cock.

On an earlier post I wrote about the book, a man was interested only in the father as a criminal who should be punished. I said the author wants to be seen. She's asking the reader to consider what a life looks like, smells like, tastes like when it has been formed in the framework of incest and rape. The man kept returning to the father. He didn't want to look at the woman's life.

Most critics have seen the author as starting in darkness and ending in darkness—as if they need to judge her as broken to prove the vileness of her ordeal. It's a commonplace to question the understandings women bring to their stories of sex as well as to question the truth of the accounts themselves. It's a commonplace publicly to disbelieve women because privately women are believed.

The author's account is not a rare thing scuttling out from under a rock. What rattled the people the author told and has rattled some critics is the story's familiarity. The extreme trauma detailed in *The Incest Diary* gains resonance not as an example of psychological perversity but as a reflection of a dominant social force. A father believing he owns the life and body of his daughter. A father cutting the genitals of his girl. A male-supremacist culture alternating intimidation with a promise of protection. The punishment of murder for disobedience. Bondage, hurting, rape, child marriage, forced allegiance to the tribe. Gee, where do these things happen? Maybe not in every white household in Greenwich, Connecticut, but in the lives of millions of girls and women right now in repressive theocracies, a reality that lends legitimacy to the actions of men like the author's father, who has not been tried for any crimes. If the stories women tell about sex were publicly acknowledged as true, what to do about everything else in the world?

What has been left for the author and what has been taken away? Based on the book's chronology, she appears to be in her early 40s. She comes across as self-reliant and profoundly alone. In the narrative, her focus is so squarely on her own sensations, other people are shadowy. Even her father is a vague presence, instrumental only to her tale of captivity and captivation.

No matter what else was happening, she excelled at school and felt an overwhelming need to protect her brother. Most evident, she has become a masterful writer, a woman alive in her flesh, and a person who does not evaluate pleasure in relationship to the way it is aroused. Pleasure is pleasure. Incest and rape are vile crimes. Her boyfriend may not be your dom. Lots of people enjoy S&M sex who were not raped as children and did not experience incest. Sexual tastes change in the course of a life, or they do not change. You can count yourself lucky if you emerge from childhood with your clitoris intact and if you get to spend at least part of your life deeply turned on.

July 6, 2018. At my mammogram today, the technician kept saying, "Breathe normal." I thought if I spoke up for the adverb, even in a gentle and non-shaming way (is that possible?), it would jinx the results of the tests. The mammogram was normal.

July 13, 2018. Can you please not stand up for a thing as a "mom." It has zero meaning to the people who want to kill your children, and it reduces the rest of us to chopped liver.

July 26, 2018. The other day Richard and I climbed onto a high cliff overlooking the English Channel. On the way up, he had a low blood sugar and was drenched in sweat. He ate glucose and bread and butter. After he recovered a little, he said he needed to sleep right there and then. We were beside a path on stubbly grass. He laid down on his rucksack and held an umbrella over his head against the sun. I opened my umbrella and stretched out beside him, and we made a little tent in the living room under the piano.

August 1, 2018. In Sidmouth we passed a small park where a woman was walking along a slack rope strung between two trees. Near her was a dog with black spots and a thick, swaying tail. Richard and I stopped to watch her. The park was bordered by hedges cut in the shapes of ancient fish and lizards—we were on the Jurassic Coast, looking out at the English Channel. The woman held her arms out to balance as she dipped her knees deeply and pivoted on the balls of her feet. The town was a time warp of seaside holiday-makers and little-England whiteness.

The tightrope walker was beautiful, about 45. The dog approached us, followed by the woman. I said, "You're wonderful." She said, "Do you want to try?" I said, "Yes," and handed my bags to Richard. She sat on the rope to steady it and keep it close to the ground. She said, "Bend the knee slightly of the leg you are standing on, look straight ahead, and raise your arms straight in the air when you lift off." The rope was flat, about three inches wide. I followed her instructions and, before wobbling off, was able to balance for moments, my left leg out to the side. She said, "Yes, you're doing it." She kept saying, "Yes." It was an activity with a spring, a trick of gravity and falling upwards I could almost taste. She was patient and told me her name. The air was salty, the evening hot. I wanted to stay with her but knew it was time to leave. You have to remind yourself sometimes to remember the rope.

THE VILLAGE VOICE

Another last goodbye

I'm sick and the phone rings. It's 4 am, and Eliot Fremont-Smith wants to edit my piece. I say, "Sure," and find the pages. I'm on the couch in the living room because I don't want to spread flu. It's 1980 and phones have those curly, umbilical cords. Eliot sounds drunk and happy. I don't feel put out the way you don't feel put out when you are in love. I'm in love with the thing we are doing. I review books weekly or almost that often for the *Voice*, and this time it's *The Transit of Venus* by Shirley Hazzard. The book will go on to win the award for best fiction from the National Book Critics Circle (NBCC), the organization founded by Eliot when he was the daily book critic for *The New York Times*. I find the writing stuffy and arch. He doesn't care. He cares about improving my sentences, and we work until morning light comes through the window. Later, does he field questions about my negative review from members of the NBCC? If so, I don't hear.

I'm at the *Voice* because of him. In 1975 he published my first piece in the paper—about the women in D.H. Lawrence's life. It ran as the lead story in the arts section, and after that I gathered more assignments, a car moving down an assembly line, trying my hand at reporting, memoir, social commentary, and comedy—sometimes all mixed together.

I'm a feminist. Here's how it happened. It's 1965, and I enter a classroom at Barnard College. Kate Millett is there, and light shoots off the bun at the back of her head. Whatever we're supposed to read we don't read. We read Beckett, Genet, Stein, and the Beats, Kate conjuring a geography of desire I want never to leave.

In 1977, Rupert Murdoch buys the *Voice*, and everyone gathers at the office on University Place and 11th Street. It's feared Murdoch will steer the paper to the right and god knows what else, so the staff agrees to form a union within the publishing wing of District 65. Murdoch will turn out to be a more hands-off owner than others, among them Leonard Stern, New Times Media, and ultimately Peter Barbey, who promised to revive the wheezing thing and managed to pull the plug in August 2018.

The union, with its Affirmative Action Committee, helps diversify future hires, establishes percentage increases on pay rates over amounts writers can wrangle for themselves, and secures benefits, including health insurance that covers "spousal equivalents"—a vaguely vegan-sounding term for your live-in honey. Could you manage on a *Voice* salary? Kind of, if, like me, you had a rent-stabilized apartment and included in your idea of a "take" free screenings, theater tickets, and books. I will go on to become a shop steward for the freelance writers. Each time contract negotiations loom, we threaten to strike and ultimately do not strike. People from all departments wear strike t-shirts and walk picket lines that give off a circus air, as passersby cheer us and flash victory signs.

I had left New York to live in East Hampton for a few years. It was not the East Hampton of self-replicating billionaires, rather the East Hampton of potato farmers and artists. For a while the man I lived with and I had a house down the road from Willem de Kooning, who was declining mentally but was still about three-fifths there. You could rent a house in the winter for the price of a city apartment—then you'd scramble to a barn or a shack when summer people rolled back in. We left the city to get away from noise. In our last place, on Bank Street, we had luckily found an apartment in the brownstone where John Cage and Merce Cunningham occupied the basement floor. Unluckily, right below us, the owner's unhappy son played amplified guitar at three in the morning.

The thing I remember most sharply from that *Voice* meeting in 1977 is not the union but bringing my dog to the office. The man I live with and I have adopted a rescue pup with a black face and white body. He is small enough to carry in a canvas tote, and out he prances into the laps of everyone there. I feel part of something I have never felt part of before, not even in the women's movement. Everyone has more cool and swagger than me. No one wants to be in love with a sure thing.

Here are some people I got to work with over the course of 25 years: Richard Goldstein, Ellen Willis, Karen Durbin, M. Mark, Stacey D'Erasmo, Ross Wetzsteon, Vince Aletti, Erika Munk, Alisa Solomon, Robert Massa, Hilton Als, Andy Hsiao, Paul Berman, Alex Cockburn, Lisa Kennedy, James Wolcott, Sylvia Plachy, Alan Stamaty, James Hamilton, Carrie Rickey, Jim Hoberman. Many more.

In 1999, I butted heads with Don Forst, who was then editor-in-chief, for speaking on the record to a reporter from *New York Press*. I spoke against cuts in editorial sections and pay for some writers and editors, and I was surprised the next day to find myself fired. *New York Press* intentionally looked for dirt on the *Voice*, and I didn't think about that. I thought I was speaking out against abuses at my paper. I didn't know Russ Smith, the founder of *New York Press*, was a political conservative. I should have known, but I was a moron about that.

Under Forst and his deputy Doug Simmons, the air at the *Voice* had taken on the tang of a sweaty jock strap, and it was time for me to go in any case. Soon the heads of most of the people I had known at the paper would roll one by one, including in time the head of Simmons. The day I was fired, I felt shot in a part of my body I could not identify, and I floated out, not feeling pain, as people claim who are actually shot. I will always be a *Voice* writer, whether or not the *Voice* exists.

Here are some pieces I got to file. In 1982, I wrote a long essay about Kafka, showing how, although he felt like a bug everywhere else in his life, he could still treat women like shit. In 1991, during the hearings for Clarence Thomas, I speculated on why more women believed Thomas than Anita Hill. The same year I wrote a defense of Pee-wee Herman, who was arrested for masturbating in a porno theater (omg!), ruminating on the hysteria stirred by the proximity of even the mention of sex to children. In 1986, I spent a month at the Carter Hotel, reporting on a homeless woman and her four children who had lived for several years in an 8' by 10' room. It was the cover story of an issue on homelessness, and because of the piece the woman and her kids were moved to an apartment in the Bronx. Later that year I wrote a 10,000 word piece about visiting Freud's house and being a Jew in Vienna, when, on vacation, I crossed paths with the presidential campaign of former Nazi Kurt Waldheim, who subsequently won.

I remember the smell of fresh ink on stacks of papers at the office and the thrill of lifting one from a red box on the street and seeing my writing there. No one changes a word without consulting you. No one urges you to write like them. We're depicted by others as a Brueghel scene of manic devils roasting each other's body parts, and it's kind of true. More keenly I remember late nights with Richard Goldstein, talking about every variant of sex. Is the show *Beauty and the Beast*, in which gorgeous Linda Hamilton hooks up with Ron Perlman, who has the face and mane of a lion(!), the first depiction of interspecies sex on TV? Yes. I remember receiving a book in the mail containing hundreds of pictures of vaginas and turning the pages, staggered by the array, while leaning against the wall of mail cubbies. I remember Guy Trebay's expanding collection of snow globes. Some contain autopsy remains dusted with glitter. (Not true.) One day I pass his cubicle with a spiky hair cut and dangly, dart-shaped earrings, and he says, "Laurie Stone, the oldest living punk."

I remember the first time I laid eyes on Alex Cockburn, some time in the mid-'70s, in the skinny elevator on University Place. He's carrying a briefcase and wearing a cashmere overcoat. There's a Peter O'Toole thing happening around his mouth, and I glance at my shoes instead of staring. Years later, when I can look at him without seeming to dissolve (although I am still dissolving), I sit in his office after we've had a few drinks and watch him compose a column due in three hours. While he continues chatting with me, out come sentences filled with lyricism, acid, erudition, and gossip about maybe Afghanistan, a country he loathes and once accused of producing "some of the worst arts and crafts ever to penetrate the Occidental world." Perhaps he's reminiscing about his father, Claud, who famously wrote in the *The Irish Times,* where he was a columnist, "Wherever there is a stink in international affairs, you will find that Henry Kissinger has recently visited."

It's 1981, and I'm on assignment for *Mademoiselle* to cover a Right-to-Life convention in Cherry Hill, New Jersey. I open my press packet to find a piece by Nat Hentoff, beloved jazz and First Amendment maven, who is also vocally opposed to abortion in the Old Testament style of Norman Mailer. Hentoff is dead meat to me and other feminists, and although he may be the only contented pawn of the right at the paper, he is not the only hand-wringing male at the feminist apocalypse.

It's 1986, and Cindy Carr writes a front-page profile of Karen Finley, extolling body art and a performance that involves Finley, playing a sociopath, shoving yams up her ass. The same year, at a time when numerous London strip clubs operate freely, London police threaten to arrest Finley if she performs nude, the message being that nudity is okay in the service of arousing men but not okay in the service of subverting that arrangement.

In the next issue of the paper Pete Hamill writes that he and the staff's other "enraged political writers" wonder how anyone can ever again take *Voice* reporting seriously. He writes, "Carr has given us a brilliant parody of (1) bohemian pretentiousness (2) the emptiness of performance art (3) a certain strain of feminism (4) the *Village Voice* itself." Then as now, I enjoy the wit of Hamill's barbs while noting how well they illustrate Finley's contention: that the erotic imagination and anxieties about sex, far from being irrelevant to public policy, actually drive it, most strikingly in the cases of AIDS and abortion.

I cover theater for the paper among other beats. During the 1980s, as New York City real estate values rocket, theaters are bought up and closed. More and more I attend solo performances in bars and clubs where your feet stick to the floor. If the haircuts and lighting are good, the performers are mostly former dancers and cannot write. If they can write, they maybe can't act or move around the stage. I know it takes comedians around seven years to create twenty good minutes of standup, and I hatch the idea of approaching comedy as theater.

In 1986 I propose a column to Karen Durbin, who is Arts editor. Usually when I enter her office, she sings all the songs from the last Lou Reed concert she's attended and follows them with a jagged memory of her midwestern childhood newly surfaced in therapy. For the only time in recorded history, she responds to a question with a single word: "Okay." And for five or so years, my column *Laughing in the Dark* alternates with Cindy Carr's column *On Edge*—a series of delirious love letters to Downtown culture and the avant-garde. The deep pleasure of writing my column and most of the pieces I produce at the *Voice* is watching art and politics rise off the streets and become a single entity. Also discovering the originality and outrageousness of brilliant women, people of color, and queers.

How did I make my way to the place I most wanted to be? It's 1971, and the man I am married to and I decide to split in the tell-all style of the times that leaves you stunned and vaguely horny for the other person because now you can miss them. Each month I hand a check for $200 to a friendly antiques dealer who owns the brownstone on Charles Street where I find a small place, plus water bugs and mice. I am working on a dissertation about Charlotte Brontë. I do not want to write a dissertation about Charlotte Brontë. I am earning just enough for food and rent by teaching two courses at Hunter College, and the rest of the time I walk. I walk past the famous bookstore on 8th Street, the men with beaky noses and floppy berets, thumbing Kerouac and Ginsberg on the lookout for girls. I walk past the White Horse Tavern, where Dylan Thomas drank himself to death. I walk along the river, beside beach grass and the hulking ruins of piers, and the smells of the tides remind me of Long Beach, where I grew up.

I'm in a consciousness-raising group and a women's writing group, and I read the *Voice*. I read Howard Smith and Jonas Mekas and Joel Oppenheimer. I read Jill Johnston and I want to write like her. I want whatever captures my attention to become a subject and to layer notes on relationships with descriptions of things outside me. Johnston is funny and seductive. She doesn't care if you like her, and she does.

One night I meet a writer I slightly know at the Lion's Head Inn. He's twice my age with a handsome face and a world-weary lean to his body. He wants to have sex with me. I want to know how to get into life. He looks at me for a moment and says, "What do you want?" I can barely choke out the words, "To write." I have already turned him down, but he's generous and I never forget what he tells me. He says, "Get on with it, then. There's not any time. There's never any time. Do not think you have time." I sit up, feeling a tightening in my chest. I say, "Okay," and something turns a few degrees, like a combination lock. Doubt doesn't dissolve, but in time I learn to ignore it.

THE CLOCK

October 13, 2018. I participated at a reading where we read short pieces in slam fashion and the sound of each separate voice became part of a thing we made together that was richer and weirder and queerer and of more different human shades than a thing any one of us could have produced alone. Afterward a friend and I went to a nearby bar and talked into the night with a beautiful bartender, whose family had come from the Dominican Republic. She wondered if she should go to Paris or Berlin to raise a child she imagined having, and we all agreed Berlin if you were alone and Paris for a kid. It was raining and warm, and the world felt beautiful to fight for.

VALERIE SOLANAS 8 WAYS

Some things that are known.

For centuries the world writes learned studies proving the biological inferiority of females and depicting them as contaminants. The world devises social and religious policy propped by the certainty of female inferiority. In 1967, Valerie Solanas self-publishes *SCUM Manifesto,* a brief, funny screed asserting that males are biologically inferior, owing to their damaged Y chromosomes. She argues that males should be treated as inferior, and her writing is pronounced crazy, perverse, and dangerous. She sells mimeographed copies on the street, charging men a dollar and women 25 cents.

At age seven, Valerie's father begins raping her on the porch swing when her mother leaves the house. She retains a memory of counting roses on the seat cushion and finding gum in her hair. By fifteen, she is homeless. During this period, she falls in love with a sailor and gives birth to a son she does not see after he is born. In 1954, at eighteen, she enrolls at the University of Maryland, where she is openly lesbian, likes talking about jazz and art, and supports herself through prostitution. After graduation, she's accepted on scholarship to a PhD program in psychology at the University of Minnesota. She doesn't complete the degree, and in 1965 sets off to be a writer in New York City.

Through Candy Darling, she gains entrée to Andy Warhol and The Factory world. Andy sees something in her he recognizes. Both are shy, ambitious, from Catholic, working class backgrounds, dubious about sex, and awkward in front of cameras. She agrees to perform in his movie, *I, a Man*, released in 1967, improvising all her dialogue. She makes him laugh. She never stops pushing him to produce her play, *Up Your Ass*. Ultimately he tires of her and misplaces the only copy of her play. In 1996, after both are dead, the play will resurface in a trunk owned by Warhol archivist Billy Name.

In 1988, Mary Harron, a researcher for the BBC, happens upon a copy of the manifesto in a London bookshop, and it takes hold of her. In 1996, the film *I Shot Andy Warhol* premieres, directed by Harron and cowritten with Daniel Minahan, featuring Lili Taylor as Solanas and Jared Harris as Warhol. In the introduction to her shooting script, Harron says Valerie's text "reached a core of anger I didn't know I possessed... It made me wonder about blighted talents, vanished possibilities, and what might be lurking in the great host of humanity we call failures."

On June 3, 1968, Valerie waits outside The Factory on Union Square, rides the elevator up with Andy, then shoots him three times with a .32 caliber pistol, wounds the art critic Mario Amaya in the hip, and tries to shoot Andy's manager, Fred Hughes. After the gun jams, she rides the elevator to the street and gives herself up to a cop at Times Square, explaining she is lonely and wants to talk to someone.

In 2006, Swedish writer Sara Stridsberg's novel *Valerie* is published to acclaim in Sweden. It depicts the life of Solanas in a collage of fictional and documentary scenes that skillfully jump between locations and time periods. In 2019, it is translated into English by Deborah Bragan-Turner and published in the US. Why the gap in time? The backward glance is always about now.

In 1988, Valerie dies of pneumonia alone in a welfare hotel in San Francisco's Tenderloin district. Stridsberg sets many scenes of her book during Valerie's final days, inventing a narrator who interviews Valerie and tries to comfort her. Valerie's body will be found days after her death, covered with maggots. Her last writings will not be saved. Close to the end of the book, the narrator says to Valerie, "I love you." Valerie says, "Fuck you."

On June 6, 1968, three days after shooting Warhol and gaining headline fame, Valerie is again whisked to the margins when Bobby Kennedy is assassinated.

On May 16, 1991 Jean-Luc Godard writes in his journal, "All you need for a movie is a girl and a gun."

Scum.

In September 1968, Maurice Girodias, the publisher of Olympia Press, rushes into print an edition of *SCUM Manifesto.* Olympia Press has published some of the great works of suppressed literature, among them: *Lolita, Candy, Naked Lunch, Story of O,* and books by Bataille and Beckett, among many others. Girodias has created the acronym, Society for Cutting Up Men, that Valerie does not endorse. He has written an introduction to the book and Paul Krassner has written an afterword. Valerie, confined in Elmhurst Psychiatric Hospital and awaiting trial for attempted murder, is unable to correct the distortions made to her work. Girodias offers to pay her legal fees, although she had come to his office to shoot him before staking out The Factory. She declines his offer.

Ti-Grace Atkinson, the president of the National Organization for Women, visits Valerie in jail and is criticized by Betty Friedan, the organization's founder. I happen to be at the meeting, and although I don't exactly know what's going on, I come to see there are women like Ti-Grace and Flo Kennedy who embody a raucous approach to feminism—in some ways modeled on the freedom of Warhol's aesthetic—where you do politics as an in-your-face throw down, not caring whom you offend, even counting offense as a plus. And there are women like Friedan, who want to make a revolution without disturbing anyone. Friedan-style women will come to dominate the public's perception of the women's movement. In time this stripe of feminist will swap the word *abortion* for the word *choice,* and while virtue-signaling women will rightly strive to include racism as a grievous social ill, they will not protest the erasure of women's rights from everyone else's agendas.

Valerie has already measured these categories in *SCUM Manifesto*, writing, "The conflict, therefore, is not between females and males, but between SCUM—dominant, secure, self-confident, nasty, violent, selfish, independent, proud, thrill-seeking, free-wheeling, arrogant females, who consider themselves fit to rule the universe, who have free-wheeled to the limits of this 'society' and are ready to wheel on to something far beyond what it has to offer—and nice, passive, accepting 'cultivated', polite, dignified, subdued, dependent, scared, mindless, insecure, approval-seeking Daddy's Girls, who can't cope with the unknown...who feel secure only with Big Daddy standing by...and with a fat, hairy face in the White House...who...can have value only...as soothers, ego boosters, relaxers and breeders..."

All you need for a movie is a girl and a gun.

I Shot Andy Warhol aims for the fragmented, verité style of Warhol's films and sends a tender love letter to the down-and-out street girls of the lesbian demi-monde. Even after Stonewall, they will remain unwelcome in many quarters. Lili Taylor plays Solanas as tough, grandiose, deranged, funny, and poignant. There are people who declare they are a genius—Gertrude Stein comes to mind—then produce enough work to qualify for recognition. What might Solanas have become if she'd had Stein's money and been less nuts?

Taylor wears floppy pants and loose jackets, camouflaging her slender body in an effort to look more formidable. She's a hustler, an aggressive panhandler prowling the East and West Village. In one of the film's most revealing scenes, she approaches Warhol at Max's Kansas City. She's been made a pariah at The Factory for staging a violent fit when she isn't paid enough attention to, and she stands on the edge of the group seated at a long table, a clique of intimates who will make no place for her. She hops from foot to foot, wanting to poke them and also will them to include her, which she knows they will not do. She's hardened and softened by the rejection. She has steeled herself to it a long time ago, but she can't control the impulse to beg, and she thrusts creased, mimeographed copies of *SCUM* at them, which they refuse, shrinking back as if she smells bad.

She asks Warhol for money. He has said he will pay her $25 to appear in a film, and she wants an advance. He says in his slow drawl that makes him sound dimwitted and shrewd at the same time, "Valerie why don't you get a job?" She says, "I can't do that, I'm an artist." He likes people who work, preferably for him, and he asks around the table if anyone has money, and no one offers any, so he withdraws a crumpled five dollar bill from his pocket and extends it to her so she will go away. She takes it with a look of shame and triumph on her face.

In another scene, she has the odd good luck to panhandle Maurice Girodias (Lothaire Bluteau), unaware he is the publisher of Olympia Press. She asks him to pay her fifteen cents to say a dirty word, and he's amused and takes her to lunch and gives her a dollar for the thirty minutes of conversation they exchange. In time he offers her a contract and an advance of $500 to write a novel in the tone of bored ease with which she describes turning tricks. He will publish a book if she will write it, and it must feel like a gun to the head. What happens when you are not a genius and someone says: *I will encourage you, I will engage with you, all you need to do is the work*?

Until this point in the film, Valerie has been appealing in her over-the-top, butch irreverence and street-rat energy, but she grows frantic and paranoid, and she stalks Girodias and Warhol. She thinks men are out to get her, and some are, but not these two men, not in the ways she imagines. She goes to shoot Girodias, but he's not in his office, so she continues to The Factory. In *Valerie*, Stridsberg's narrator brilliantly distills the next moments in the form of an address to Valerie: "You hold your life in your hand. . . . *The moment you shoot Andy Warhol, you throw away all possibility of being someone other people listen to, the only thing you dream about, the writer, artist, revolutionary, psychoanalyst, rebel.*" The bullets damage Warhol's liver, spleen, esophagus, and lungs. He never completely recovers physically, and afterward suffers from a lasting terror she will return to finish him off.

At the end of the film, slender books with orange spines are stacked on a table, and people are buying the Girodias edition of *SCUM*. I remember coming upon a copy in a kiosk on a Greek island. I read it on a boat and thought Solanas's understanding of the sexual double standard was as clear as the absence of the emperor's new clothes. Why couldn't everyone see it? *SCUM* was one of two books in English I could find on the island. The other was *The Moonstone* by Wilkie Collins, another mystery I enjoyed.

A modest proposal.

From *SCUM Manifesto*: "SCUM is impatient; SCUM is not consoled by the thought that future generations will thrive; SCUM wants to grab some thrilling living for itself. And, if a large majority of women were SCUM, they could acquire complete control of this country within a few weeks simply by withdrawing from the labor force, thereby paralyzing the entire nation. Additional measures, any one of which would be sufficient to completely disrupt the economy and everything else, would be for women to declare themselves off the money system, stop buying, just loot and simply refuse to obey all laws they don't care to obey. The police force, National Guard, Army, Navy and Marines combined couldn't squelch a rebellion of over half the population, particularly when it's made up of people they are utterly helpless without."

"Ten for a fuck, five for a blow job, two for a hand job. No kissing. No fingers. No licking."

If comedy does not contain displaced anger, it won't be funny. Ti-Grace Atkinson called Valerie "a heroine of the women's movement." Valerie called the women's movement "a civil disobedience luncheon club." In 1969, after learning of the moon landing, Valerie said, "Well, if they could put one man on the moon, why not all of them?"

When she first met Andy and said she was a writer, he jokingly offered her a job as a typist at The Factory. Last night I worked a party at a venue. It was understaffed, and my partner and I were moving for ten hours. At the end, a male guest needed to dispose of dry ice in a pot. I brought him into the bathroom where there was a sink, and he dumped out the ice and ran hot water over it. When I returned to the sink, I saw he had left all the bits of fruit and candy at the bottom for me to clean up, although there was a hole for waste right beside the sink. At Valerie's arraignment in Manhattan Criminal Court on June 3, she was asked by the judge, "Do you need a lawyer?" She said, "I need a kiss."

You hold your life in your hand.

The narrator of *Valerie* imagines Valerie with her mother and former lovers, scenes Solanas did not document. Skip these sections. The book comes alive when we hear Valerie's voice (often extracted from *SCUM Manifesto*) and when the narrator dwells not on Valerie's motives but on the things she did, lining up moments like exhibits at a trial that has no verdict. Valerie's position on prostitution: "charging for rape." Drugs: She used "amphetamine, cocaine, heroin, benzodiazepine, and LSD." Her recollection of her early days at The Factory: "I liked being there so much, I wanted to be one of those needle junkies and fag-whores who sat along the walls, sweating and mumbling and waiting for Andy to come and make art out of them. They were very happy days. Andy laughed at everything I said. I read aloud from the manifesto… I wanted The Factory to swallow me up forever." Valerie is tried in June 1969 and sentenced to two years in prison in addition to the year she has served for the attempted murder of Andy Warhol and his associates. Stridsberg's narrator again: "What is regarded as an extremely lenient penalty is probably due to Andy Warhol's refusal to appear in court, the demonstrations outside the courthouse every day in support of your release from hospital, and not least Florynce Kennedy's blazing defense."

The book skillfully situates Valerie's life in an historical framework, reminding us, for example, that in 1955 the Hiroshima Maidens arrived in New York City for free reconstructive surgery and in 1953 nuclear testing occurred on Bikini Atoll and the Rosenbergs were executed by electric chair, a fate Valerie might have faced, according to New York State law at the time, had she killed Warhol instead of wounding him.

And the novel is at its strangest—most murky? most mysterious?—when Stridsberg pits her Daddy's Girl narrator against her own private Valerie, who always comes out on top, telling the narrator to quit romanticizing her and instead do something useful: "Stop in the subway and talk to the psychotic hookers. Don't walk away when she starts raving about nothing... Ask what she has in her notes, if you're so interested in dying crack whores. Visit hostels, mental hospitals, drug ghettos, red-light districts, jails. The world's out there waiting for you, baby. The material is called SHE'S EVERYWHERE."

Abused crackpot with 15 minutes of fame.

In an essay in *Full Stop*, published on May 21, 2019, Chavisa Woods compares Valerie's status in social memory to the status of male artist-felons, among them William Burroughs, who in 1951 shot his wife Joan Vollmer dead in Mexico, and Norman Mailer, who in 1960 stabbed his wife Adele Morales in the chest, nearly piercing her heart. Pablo Neruda raped a "servant" while visiting her country as a diplomat. Charles Bukowski is on video, Woods reports, "kicking and punching his girlfriend during an interview about his writing, and was said to have been physically abusive to multiple female partners." French Marxist philosopher Louis Althusser strangled his wife to death in an act of cold-blooded murder. Woods does not include the unwitnessed murder in 1986 by sculptor Carl Andre of his wife artist Ana Mendieta, who plunged from a 33-story window, following a violent argument witnesses heard. Andre said they were arguing about his greater artistic success.

Burroughs was not arrested, and he left Mexico. Mailer claimed that if he had not stabbed Adele, he would have gotten cancer from repressed rage. He walked away from the stabbing with a suspended sentence for third-degree assault and spent fifteen days in a psychiatric ward. Neruda wrote about the rape as a no-big-deal episode in his memoir *I Confess That I Have Lived* (1974). In the Wikipedia bio for Althusser, Woods notes, the murder of his wife is mentioned in the last paragraph and only in the context of his mental illness: "Althusser's life was marked by periods of intense mental illness. In 1980, he killed his wife, the sociologist Hélène Rytmann, by strangling her." In 1988, Carl Andre was tried and acquitted of Mendieta's murder on the grounds of "reasonable doubt."

All these men continued to work, publish, and collect praise. Adele Morales did not press charges. When I lived next door to her, I wondered but did not ask her why, after the stabbing, she spent two more years with Norman before leaving him. In 2014, I joined a protest organized by Christen Clifford against a giant retrospective of Carl Andre's work at Dia art gallery. Similar protests dogged the show as it traveled the country and abroad.

Does anyone still read Mailer? Woods quotes a passage from *Advertisements for Myself* (1959) that sounds like something Valerie might have written as a parody of male rage: "I have nothing to say about any of the talented women who write today... I do not seem able to read them. Indeed, I doubt if there will be a really exciting woman writer until the first whore becomes a call girl and tells her tale... I can only say that the sniffs I get from the ink of the women are always fey, old-hat, Quaintsy Goysy, tiny, too dykily psychotic, crippled, creepish, fashionable, frigid, outer-Baroque, maquillé in mannequin's whimsy, or else bright and stillborn." Dykily psychotic! A new bar to aim for.

Every backward glance is about now.

Warhol was famous, and he was a man, and Valerie wanted him to help her, and she went for him the way hustlers go for you, with a hand out and a push, without embarrassment and nothing but embarrassment, with bravado that is not earned and is everywhere on the landscape of advertising The Factory fed on. The culture of branding and self-promotion and marketing is Valerie shaking you down at an ATM. At the end of the '70s, she's sighted at Tompkins Square Park and on St. Mark's Place: hungry, dirty, alone, selling sex and the manifesto, threatening to kill Kate Millett and to throw lye in the face of Robin Morgan because they defended her.

SCUM Manifesto is a performance of Valerie's personality, not a kit for murdering famous men. "I didn't want to kill him. I wanted him to pay attention to me. Talking to him was like talking to a chair," she is quoted as saying when asked for the umpteenth time why she shot Andy Warhol. ("The Radical Possibilities of Valerie Solanas," by Breanne Fahs, *Feminist Studies*, Fall 2008) *SCUM* is a manifestation of rage few people want to believe exists in the female heart. I would say it exists in the heart of every woman who has lived in a body interpreted as female. I would say it's small potatoes beside the rage aimed at women that goes unremarked on because it's considered so ordinary in the codes of every religion and in the writings of man after man after man.

Reading Woods, I was at first uncertain about the comparison she was making between writers and artists of considerable achievement and Solanas, who wrote clumsily and very little. But who attracts us now, and who do we care to think about? For the vast part, when I read the books of men—it doesn't matter what century—I find I do not exist in them, nor does anyone like me exist in them, and it is like reading the literature of a lost civilization.

THE CLOCK

August 6, 2018. People ask me about plastic surgery with curiosity and distaste. It's like watching a cooking show when you have decided not to eat.

August 18, 2018. I have been spending several days in Greenfield, Mass., visiting a friend who has lived in the town for decades. When I arrived, she showed me the encampment that homeless people had recently established on the central green, and my friend, a lawyer, was interested in the fact that residents were not protesting their presence. The police and other officials have said as of now they have no plans to remove or re-situate them. Every Saturday a green market banks the central square, and today the market tents and homeless tents peacefully coexisted. Some among the homeless sat at picnic tables in the square, smoking and sipping from bottles. A couple had a screaming fight. I followed them, concerned the man might hurt the woman. She was loud, and he kept turning to get away from her. She followed him and tugged at him. He was trying not to hurt her, it seemed to me, and they disappeared down a side street.

I talked to a woman at one of the market stands selling bags of popcorn. I asked what she felt about the homeless encampment. She shrugged and said she wasn't sure. I said, "Massachusetts ranks highest among the states in opposition to Trump. I think if Hillary were president and we were not living amid so much hatred of people in need, the residents of Greenfield might be asking the police and government to intervene. Now, though, I think people cannot bear to align themselves with the rounding up and herding of people in trouble. There might be an empathy dividend." She said, "Could be." Then a woman bought three giant bags of popcorn, and the seller said, "She must be having a party."

August 21, 2018. I find it moving to learn that Leonard Bernstein was buried with the score of Mahler's 5th Symphony.

August 22, 2018. I read that the word "vagina" is being discontinued as insensitive to women who don't have vaginas. The preferred term is "front hole." It's still okay to say "penis" whenever you want to, however, although on my post writer Mark Givens offers the possibility it may in time be referred to as "front stick."

August 27, 2018. Yesterday on WQXR, the DJs mentioned it was National Dog Day and also National Women's Equality Day. Dogs called the station to protest the invidious comparison.

August 30, 2018. The lasting regrets of my life have been things I did not buy. A gold ring with a fiery opal. A watch in Paris with Japanese characters.

September 3, 2018. On our way to Otto's in Germantown, my friend and I stopped at a posh jewelry store to get out of the heat. The store was part of the Brooklyn-hipster creep up the Hudson Valley. I saw a ring. It was gold with a slash of a stone across the top, a bit of crystal, maybe, and I tried it on, and it looked good. It looked great, and I wanted it. I started to imagine how much I would pay. I started to think about things I would forgo and food I would not eat in order to have it. I tried the ring on several fingers and found the one where it looked best, and you know where this is going, because rings slip out of my grasp in reality the way they do in other people's dreams.

The woman who worked there was tall and slender and very beautiful with thick chestnut hair and peachy skin. She floated over, and I asked how much the ring cost. She said, "$4,500. It's the most expensive piece in the store." She called the slash of stone some kind of diamond. A broken glass shard diamond? I had stopped listening.

September 4, 2018. "We would be honored to have you," wrote David Remnick in his invitation to white nationalist Steve Bannon, inviting him to appear at *The New Yorker* literary festival, a decision that would have warmed the hearts of famed supporters of the Vichy government in occupied France: Maurice Chevalier, Coco Chanel, (who took a German lover and schemed to regain control over her company from the Jewish family that had taken a majority interest in the 1920s), Sacha Guitry and Jean Cocteau (who happily socialized and cooperated with the Germans, even writing a fatuous essay comparing Hitler's court sculptor Breker to Michelangelo). These notes are from David Bell's review in *The New Republic* of *And the Show Went On: Cultural Life in Nazi-Occupied Paris* by Alan Riding. After many writers withdrew from the festival, *The New Yorker* canceled Bannon.

September 6, 2018. The psychoanalyst who took me to his bed when I was fourteen gave me books to read. One was *The Frog Pond,* an autobiographical novel by Joyce MacIver, a pseudonym, about a woman attracted to violent, sadistic men, some of them her analysts. I remember becoming aroused. I love that language can do this.

September 8, 2018. I remember a French woman who took pills with the intention of dying. While she was unconscious, her dog chewed off her nose, lips, and chin. She awoke without pain and covered in blood. Doctors transplanted another woman's face onto hers—another suicide, as it happened. She appeared on TV. You could see stitches, but she didn't look that strange. She had been ready to die, but after she awoke, she fought hard to prepare for her surgeries, as if they gave her a reason to live. I thought it was the company of others. So many people wanting to help her were suddenly there.

September 11, 2018. A few days after the planes hit the towers, I was included in a group of volunteers escorted to Ground Zero. A friend of mine knew a young woman who was an Anglican priest. She had a posh parish on the Upper East Side, and 9/11 gave her something grittier to do with her time. She was English and beautiful and able to be earnest and witty at the same time because of the accent and being English. She had special access to the site because she was delivering last rites over the remains that were found. She wore a white vestment when she said the last words, looking down at dusty rubble and wreckage.

We were taken to Trinity Church and from there to Bouley Bakery to prepare meals for the workers at the site. I had never been to Bouley Bakery, but I knew how to work in a professional kitchen. I remember a long stainless steel table where strudel dough was extruded from a machine. It was enormous. It could have produced enough strudel for the entire city. We weren't making strudel. We worked all night until the sun came up. I was able to return to make food on other days.

My friend who knew the Anglican priest was a journalist. We weren't tired at the end of the long shift, rather a little giddy and wobbly. For a while we stood outside the fenced area of devastation and looked at it changing colors in the reddish glow of the rising sun. Workers in hard hats moved around. There were vans from the Red Cross in the streets, dispensing the food we had helped prepare. A certain kind of camaraderie forms around disasters, and all of New York City was like that for a while. I loved my friend especially that night, and the feeling of our time together there has stayed with us.

September 13, 2018. Adam Driver was one of the most compelling elements in *Girls*: the sexually driven, wild man you are never going to stay with, who likes children.

September 16, 2018. I am remembering a man who touched and kissed me in ways that scared me. I am thinking about this in light of the misstep by Ian Buruma to publish an account in *The New York*

Review of Books by Jian Ghomeshi, a man accused by more than twenty women of uninvitedly choking, suffocating, punching, and violently penetrating them (but no penis and no conviction).

The man I am remembering is good looking enough, with thick, red hair and an athletic build. Maybe we have come back to my apartment after a meal. It's 1970. My apartment is small. Barely a mattress and dresser fit in the bedroom. As soon as he touches me, I know something is wrong. In those days, if I drank at all, it was one glass of vermouth. He presses his mouth against mine and pushes me against a wall. He wears a rough half-smile, as if he knows a secret about me. Does he encircle my neck? It's not easy to get him to leave, and in those minutes that may stretch into an hour, I am aware I am not in control. I use words that are not mine. I whisper and say, "please."

Nothing that happens with him sexually has been perceivable before coming to the apartment. Maybe I get him to leave because I know his cousin. I don't tell her. If she asks about him, I say we aren't right for each other. I wish I had told her. I looked at the episode as a close call, and it changed nothing I can put my finger on about the way I interacted with men or approached sex afterward. I considered it a fluke along with other incidents I didn't like to believe could happen to me. I didn't want to be stopped in going for the things I wanted.

September 16, 2018. Why the erotic imagination matters in discussions of public policy: Most men who consider themselves progressive don't get hard at the thought of white supremacy. Opposing racism is a groin-free zone. Men get hard at the idea of male supremacy. Not all men. Not all the time. Look at the accounts men offer about their confusion about sex—what desire is, what attraction is, what they are supposed to do, what they want to do. It's because men can get hard—or sometimes get hard at the idea of male supremacy—that absolute bodily sovereignty for women can remain a fuzzier domain for them than racial equality. And the women who militate against their own freedom and independence? The same erotics—the erotics of being number two—color their inclinations as well.

September 17, 2018. I am loving Maggie Gyllenhaal in *The Deuce* and the show's look back at the Times Square where everybody crossed paths, the movie theaters where you watched *Midnight Cowboy* and outside saw the same characters cruising the streets, where the theater floors stuck to your feet and the never-dark twilight fought with images on the screen. In *The Deuce,* I love the feminism streaking the world of sex workers and porno film makers. I remember women from Coyote at a meeting I went to in the '60s or '70s, the organization that championed rights for sex workers. The name Coyote was an acronym for "call off your old tired ethics." The women had curly hair and ironic expressions.

September 18, 2018. Takeaway from Brett Kavanaugh and his defenders: *It's not my personal fault, since it's okay everywhere in the world to treat women like garbage.* He has a point.

September 20, 2018. Regarding the unseating of Ian Buruma as editor-in-chief of *The New York Review of Books*: When collective disgust has an impact on garden variety misogyny, it's termed the mob rule of social media. When ordinary misogyny governs every aspect of society, it's termed the course of reason and civilized persuasion. Had Buruma been as cluelessly racist as he was cluelessly sexist, not a single self-described political progressive would have objected to his unseating on the grounds of mass hysteria and overkill. His unseating would have been seen as fitting and long overdue. On both the Right and the Left, calling attention to sexism is the thing that is bothersome, not the sexism itself.

September 20, 2018. You live with the details of sexual predation for the rest of your life. I have written many times and in different forms about André Glaz, the psychoanalyst who molested me sexually when I was fourteen, began having sex with my cousin when she was eleven, sexually molested many other children he treated, and engaged in sex with many women who came to him for therapy. He did not ruin my life. He did not penetrate me with his penis. It happened two times in the course of one day when I was at his house in the country. The second time I was able to stop him. He touched me everywhere. I can feel his touch. It did not dull my response to pleasure. It shaped the way I see the world.

At the time it happened, I told no one. The first person I told was the boy I would marry when I was nineteen. By then André was no longer in my life but was alive and remained in the lives of members of my family. I did not tell them until years later. Each time I tell this story, the world I tell it in is a little different.

September 20, 2018. It used to be legal to racially segregate drinking fountains, bathrooms, and swimming pools. It should be illegal to sexually segregate the bodies of women, understood to be contaminating agents, in the practices of all religions and other social organizations. Were this the case, rape culture would look less like ordinary life.

September 21, 2018. In a post I wrote: I think we are witnessing the nervous breakdown at the end of masculinist culture in the form of a zombie apocalypse of very ugly men, leaking slimy fluids, in agonized poses. A young woman reposted my statement and added, with a smiley face, "Of course you mean 'ugly on the inside.'" I said, "No, I meant it as I wrote it." She said the disability movement strongly opposed the word "ugly," used in any context. I told her I didn't care. I didn't want to be corrected, cleaned up, or advised on my posts. She deleted the post and unfriended me. This is neo-good-girl-itis—the need felt by females to look virtuous and to correct others. The more people are afraid to use language, at the risk of causing offense, the harder it is to think their own thoughts. This is not a time to get dumber and more timid.

September 26, 2018. Enough with the "as a privileged, cis-gendered, white, abashed, mortified for existing, willing to sever an artery to feed endangered bats" qualifications. By the way, you're not that privileged if you have to talk like this.

September 26, 2018. I found *Jane Fonda in Five Acts* (HBO) startling and moving. I am thinking about Fonda's activism, the many years she spent living on the front lines of progressive and antiwar activism, how much this meant to the times and expressed them. How much the activism allowed her to feel known to herself. It was a joy to relive those eras that seem, in comparison to our moment, joyously free of cynicism and despair. I love her son's recollections of life in the Hayden/Fonda household, the flood of people in the life of this child that allowed his parents to be better parents to him than Jane says she was able to be to her daughter, born when she was living in France with Roger Vadim and did not have a community to help her or a husband who was as hands-on as Hayden appears to have been. On camera in the documentary, Fonda now exudes a governing lostness and sweetness. Clips from her early performances in *They Shoot Horses, Don't They?* and *Klute* are stunning.

September 28, 2018. People have been writing the past few days about the trauma of publicly detailing sex crimes and other forms of assault and harassment. They have been saying in some cases it's futile because of the current climate of hostility expressed by the GOP government. It is not futile. I remember attending a meeting of Red Stockings. It would have been before 1971 because by then abortion was legal in New York state. It became legal because of this kind of feminist pressure. At the meeting, women were recounting their abortions and I think also rapes. Sharing detailed revelations about rape and other violence was part of the practice of those times, and it accumulated in the public conversation, saying: "No, you don't have it right. Here is what happened and still happens. Do not think you know what you do not know."

September 30, 2018. A suggestion was going around Facebook for women to swap out their pictures for a black box—a symbolic demonstration of what the absence of women would mean. I thought, no. A black box reminds me of a burka. Orthodox Jews also impose burkas with eye slits on women. Why as a protest would women think it's a good idea to disappear? If you want to slip into something black, might I suggest the little black number Audrey Hepburn wore in *Breakfast at Tiffany's*?

October 1, 2018. The negative voices on my feed of white men of an age that used to call themselves Marxists and perhaps still do sound the same way they sounded 50 years ago when they had mustaches and long sideburns and would lean in a corner holding a juice glass of wine, trying to pick you up by telling you, "The women's movement, it will never fly, it will never go anywhere, it's a joke."

October 5, 2018. There is no such thing as a backlash. The backlash is always the front lash.

October 31, 2018. I'm reposting this poem I love by the great David Daniel.

"The Joke"

The skeleton, my son says,
Can't cross the road because
It doesn't have the guts—
Which explains, perhaps, why
It's still at the edge of our yard
Looking out across the road, into the dark.
I'm just kidding—
You see, it's us by the roadside,
Our bones the wind whistles,
And the darkness beyond:
That's ours also.

November 4, 2018. Thoughts aroused by Dan Chiasson's piece about the letters of Sylvia Plath in *The New Yorker*: I am struck by the apology made by Frieda, the daughter of Sylvia Plath and Ted Hughes, for the brutality of her father toward her mother, who killed herself when

Frieda was three. This is Frieda commenting on a letter Plath wrote to her former shrink, detailing a beating by Hughes she says caused her to miscarry. Writes Frieda: "What, I asked myself, would qualify as a physical beating? A push? A shove? A swipe? The assault had not warranted a mention in [an] earlier letter where my mother had written 'There was no apparent reason to miscarry'. But of course, now that the relationship was disintegrating, what woman would want to paint her exiting husband in anything other than the darkest colours."

Frieda, your mother worked her ass off to paint her relationship to Hughes in the cheeriest colors for as long as she could as a boast about her great catch. The knowledge she quickly gained about the shittiness of marriage to a man like Hughes, who thought mainly about Hughes, while she was managing two small kids and an ambition like hers, this knowledge made her feel like a failure in a game she did not live long enough to know was rigged. Plath was turned on by Hughes. She thought she was also supposed to be turned on by the role of wife to a man like that, and it wasn't sexy. In the photograph published with the Chiasson piece, Hughes is stretched out on a cream colored divan with his shoes on. He isn't thinking about who is going to wash the cover. It isn't going to be him. He may not have known how to wash the cover of a divan or to locate a clitoris, a capacity which, according to Plath, improved after he began sleeping with the woman he would leave her for.

Chiasson says of Plath's writing: "Now I often teach her poems, but rarely read them aloud; it is too absurd to hear a man say the lines, 'I rise with my red hair/And I eat men like air.'" I don't think it would sound absurd for a man to say these words. I think it would be great to hear a man inhabit the consciousness that could produce them. These lines are braggy. Plath was braggy about many things and then bluntly reversed herself. I think Chiasson doesn't want these words on his lips because they are girly. He doesn't want to have girl in his mouth or coming out of his mouth.

November 8, 2018. Imagine what would have happened, how the world would have responded, what terms would have been applied, if the actions, the statements, the gestures, the facial expressions, the hairdo, the clothes, the body shape of the thing that is occupying the White House belonged to a female instead of a male.

November 13, 2018. “If a writer were a free man and not a slave, if he could write what he chose, not what he must, if he could base his work on his own feeling and not on convention, there would be no plot, no comedy, no tragedy, no love interest or catastrophe in the accepted style.”—Virginia Woolf, quoted in a wonderful piece about walking by Kathryn Davis. Pretend Woolf said “free woman.” I can’t fathom why she did not, except most humans in her time thought people who wrote were male, even a female writer.

November 14, 2018. I watch hummingbirds at the feeder. One perches on the handle while the other dives at it for reasons that are a blur. They spin and fight, arriving together and leaving together, and no one gets to eat. I don’t know when I lost interest in why things are the way they are. From time to time I find a letter, an email, a phone number from a person I sent love to and have forgotten exists. Today I picked a grapefruit from a tree, cut it the French way, as if to serve it to someone else, and ate it. I don’t remember when I formed a romantic image of traveling light, emotions all you need to carry. Richard and I watched *High Maintenance,* and you think pot takes the edge off what’s missing. The stoned guy reminds me of a man I once loved who was mostly absent. The hummingbirds are so into each other they can’t be bothered to eat.

November 19, 2018. The first episode of *My Brilliant Friend* aired on HBO last night. I have not read Elena Ferrante’s books. These comments are about the TV series. At the center of the life of every female is not a man, not a child, not parents, not siblings, but a female best friend. It is the person you sit next to on the bus, or you are chosen for her kickball team, and you feel you never want to leave. You will figure out a way to marry her. You will sleep in her bed. You will look for her for the rest of your life. She will leave you. You will outgrow her. You will find versions of her. Female friendship is your one true north, and it's maddening and funny because no one depicts it. No one is willing to express the endless life of female friendship because part of its power is that it is a secret every female knows.

The girls are beautifully cast. The way they eye each other before the bolder one, who is also the more socially awkward one, makes a move. Once they join hands, the bond is set. The bond is to escape the condition of being female. The girls understand it as a condition. It is the defining quality of girlness to know that girlness is a thing you are born into and must escape. You need a partner. You need an army, but a partner is what you have if you are lucky. In Naples a woman-future is opera all the time. Loud and sad and worn out by thirty. There are male humans, but male humans are registered only in so far as they are or may be instrumental to how girls will leave the condition of girlness.

In a breathtaking sequence, Elena, writing as the older author looking back at her childhood, recalls a dream in which, suddenly, millions of beetles are released from sewers and fissures in the land and swarm the streets, scale the walls of the houses, and cover the bedding of sleepers, diving into the open mouth of a woman asleep on her back. The beetles with their hard carapaces and endless capacity to replicate are, collectively, the feeling of the female condition. When the girls clasp hands, they have begun the great adventure of their lives, which is to leave the understandings of other people and reinvent everything.

November 20, 2018. *My Brilliant Friend,* Episode 2. I am struck by the foreground of female rivalry set against a backdrop of male violence and the atmosphere of general terror it produces in the community. Fathers are supposed to rule their households, even if they don't want to. Girls in the mainly lower ranks of these villagers are not supposed to be educated. Class and sexism combine to confine a girl to the role of drone in the family of birth and later in the family she makes as a wife. The female teacher of the girls mounts the only opposition to these values, and although she tries to steel

Lila's mother to intervene on behalf of her brilliant child, she has to relent, seeing the effort is futile.

Lila's father will throw her out a window after she says she will take the test to enter middle school without his permission. Her arm is broken in the fall. It's a horrifying moment. The women gather around the child, who downplays the injury. The women, including Lila's mother, say, "She fell." Lila is going to exit her circumstance by any means necessary, and it kills her that Lenu, who is devoted to her, has been given permission by her father to take the test. Lila devises a scheme to sabotage Lenu by enticing her to cut school and walk to the ocean. The scheme doesn't work, and Lenu understands the betrayal, but she also understands its twisted source. It is the logic of: If I can't go, then why should you? And Lenu deals with another version of this with her mother, who seethes with resentment at the way Lenu's father dotes on her. The mother can't bear the disparity between her fate and the possibility that her daughter will not replicate her life, and in their interaction we see the machinery of sexism working inside women.

Lenu's mother goads her husband to beat Lenu for cutting class, taunting him to show he's a man. If the world of female roles is not a fixed thing, if it can be altered, then Lenu's mother did not have to forfeit her own hopes for her life. The thought that her own renunciation wasn't necessary is unbearable, and all her energy will go to propping up the system that will keep them both down.

There are moments of beauty along the way. Lenu's father beats her but insists she will take the test, and Lila's brother stands up to their father and says he will pay for his sister to go to school because, "Everyone knows she's the smartest person in the village." He fails, of course, but it is a gorgeous gesture, as is the kindness toward Lila of another boy, whose intelligence has been thwarted and who has been tricked into hawking produce on the street.

We see Lila through her actions and the ferocity of her calculations that she shares only with Lenu. She does not need Lenu in order to carry our her plans, but she wants an accomplice and an audience. Lenu needs Lila to become herself, so she forgives the betrayal. She does not want to know what she has learned about Lila, but she does know, and the knowledge will peek out from what obscures it from time to time.

The episode is extraordinary in its complexity and in the way it remains focused on the girls trying to become themselves. They read *Little Women* over and over until the pages become grimy. It's an act of enormous rebellion, for them as dangerous as scaling a steep mountain. We're inside Lenu's consciousness. This is the mind we can penetrate, partly because she is telling the story, sometimes in the voiceover of the adult writer. Also because Lenu is not fixed and rigid as Lila is said to be. We can see this as well. Lenu is the collector of ambivalence that will not be resolved.

November 22, 2018. Today a friend told me a story about a writer he knew. The writer had written a novel that was accepted for publication at a trade house, and he was told all was well except for one element. The story included a trans character and the publisher wanted to send the book to a "Sensitivity Reader." The author, who is not a trans person, did not like the idea of being vetted in this way and took the book to a different house.

I wondered about other ways books could be vetted for "sensitivity." Did the publisher send books about women written by men to female "sensitivity" readers? What about books about men written by women? Were there "sensitivity readers" for books about race, religion, nationality, forms of trauma the author had not experienced? What possible good could any of this do for writing, publishing, the issue itself of calming the frizz of bias and phobia?

Yesterday a friend used the term *pussy whipped* in a post. I feel a current of rage go through me when I hear this term as well as the words *douche, douchebag, pussy* (for weakling), *wuss* (variant of puss), and *cunt* compared to pieces of shit. I did not ask anyone to stop using these terms, not because I want to keep hearing them but because I don't think social change happens through censorship and "sensitivity harassment."

Every time I feel a surge of rage, I have been harmed a little. Disagreement is not trauma, but the free flow of sexist and misogynist language tears at the safety and freedom of all women all the time. It does do harm. The remedy is not restricting language and the crazy and at times poetically weird and unexpected meanings language stirs.

Back to the book publisher. If someone wanted to vet a book or even an article or story of mine through a "Sensitivity Reader," I would pull it. In fact something similar happened to me in 2016 at the Columbia University radio station WKCR. How does a society designate a term hate speech? Are the underpinnings almost always economic? Meaning, is the impulse to censor or moderate language stirred by fear of an economic backlash by consumers? Is that what the book publisher feared, a backlash of disapproval about a non-trans person depicting a trans character?

I want the freedom to explain how it feels to be demeaned by assumptions about female humans. I also don't want anything to police or restrict your freedom to say the things that piss me off.

November 26, 2018. *My Brilliant Friend,* Episode 3. The episode opens with Lenu discovering blood in the toilet. She thinks she is going to die, and she is right. Another girl explains it's her period and it means she can get pregnant. Lila has moved away from Lenu. There are girls who work in shops and girls who go to school. The romance of childhood is, *How does life work?*

By now the girls are thirteen or so, and life is a bird on a dusty road. Lenu doesn't know how to study without Lila. She doesn't know how to live without the romance of her relationship to this girl, who knows the grammar of existence. You have to start with the verb, she will explain to Lenu, showing her how to master Latin, as they sit side by side on a curb in the dark. It's the tenderest and most beautiful scene in the episode, the girls finding their way back to each other.

Lenu has discovered that Lila is secretly reading her way through the library that has opened in the town, signing the names of other members of her family to the cards, in order to borrow more books. What do you do when you have found and lost the most interesting human being you have ever known? The one who finds cracks of light in cinderblock walls? You do everything in your power to win her back, and you measure the space inside you she inhabits.

Lenu's face has broken out in acne. She thinks she is ugly and that Lila is beautiful. Lila gives off sexual power with the force she hides. She's a bit scary to people, and she uses it to stay separate. Lenu's breasts are developing, and boys are eyeing her. Two confront her in a toilet and one offers her ten lire to show him her breasts. She holds out her hand and takes the money, curling her fingers around the coin. You can't tell what she's thinking when she lifts her sweater. She looks blank, like a sex worker, waiting for the moment to pass into another when she will spend the money on a pastry. She is testing what her body can provide. In a voiceover, the adult Lenu believes she was channeling Lila in that moment. We think she is also testing herself in the realm of boys and what they want.

One of the genius aspects of the show is the way it forces male viewers to identify with the female characters. There is no other place to go. In the entire episode, the only male who is kind to Lenu is an elderly male librarian. When her grades are failing, her father loses patience with her. Other males form a backdrop of large and small aggressions to each other and to girls. The rich boys drive around in a car and compel a poorer girl from the town to get in. She doesn't want to. Everyone watches and lets it happen. Lila is enraged and calls it an "abduction."

Later, when these same boys will harass Lenu and one grabs her arm, breaking her bracelet, Lila will hold a knife at his throat and threaten to stab him if he touches her again. We can see the boy is turned on by Lila's lack of fear. Fear is the medium the girls exist in. There is only one path out of this world for Lenu, and it is by following the crumbs laid down by Lila, who may not, herself, get out.

November 27, 2018. *My Brilliant Friend,* Episode 4. There's a Shakespearean feel to several scenes in this episode. A Sharks and Jets thing as factions in the town assemble, and sex, history, and politics enter the lives of the girls. People stop in the street to confer about power. People have to talk to each other in person because there is no other way to communicate, and it's sexy to talk with bodies proximate in time and space. Lila is in her father's shop, scheming to get rich with her brother through their secret shoe business. Money is flowing into the town, and the girls learn how the rich got powerful as black marketeers during the war and how they remain in power through their associations with mafia types.

In the rise of the pushed-around poor against the cut-throat rich, the sexes join, with Lila at the hub. All the boys want her body and mind. It's the first time in the series we get to see more of the males and their complexity. Even Lenu's father comes alive as he tours his daughter through Naples, meeting people in the streets and seeming happy and chatty as he shows her off. She's never seen him this way, and she finally beholds the sea she did not get to that time the girls ventured out and retreated before they could arrive.

Lenu has started high school, and at first she's shy and unsteady without Lila. She makes a vow to herself to study hard. She needs to outdo Lila at something, Lila who has already finished reading the *Aeneid* in Greek. Lenu earns an A for her translation but not before the teacher questions whether she has plagiarized the work. "No," she says sharply. Naples is teeming. It's a real city, and it's wonderful to see Lenu wandering around, learning to be unprotected. She has this on Lila. Their rivalry isn't something to see as a corruption of love. We fall in love with the people we want to be, at least in some ways, and as we rub against them, the edges of our separate selves blend a little.

The episode is called "Dissolving Margins," and it represents many things about alliances of power in the town as well. Lila explains to Lenu, "We don't know anything about power." She is saying they have to study the world as much as books, and several of the boys in their circle have knowledge they need. Lila will go anywhere to get a leg up on fear. She says that knowledge will help them control the fear they live in. That may or may not be true in her case. It may only be something she wants to believe.

Lenu may be a better student of Lila's words than Lila can be. She has attracted one of the rich, thug boys, the one she threatened to stab as she held a knife to his throat. He's coming for her, and he has the added challenge for Lila of being beautiful, and we all know where beauty leads. Maybe beauty is more implacable than who owns the means of production in the town. In any case, every ingredient that makes a Shakespeare tragedy and comedy and history play is in this brilliant episode that flies at us like the fireworks war in the final scene, joyous and terrifying, everyone awake.

December 3, 2018. *My Brilliant Friend,* Episode 5. I watch the show with my hands over my mouth and my eyes ready to shut against the violence that erupts. What is a man? No one cares. They can kill you, and they're uninteresting. I hate this episode. I could not stop watching it.

There are too many men in this chapter and things men say and do that encircle women. Lila is a fly in a spider's web. The more she buzzes, the more the silk tightens. The men want her aliveness inside them, and then they want it to stop. She's fifteen. Who asks a girl of fifteen to get married? She's afraid of the world, and somehow Lenu is not. The thing that brought tears to my eyes is when Lenu tells Lila she is leaving for the summer. She has a chance to escape and swim in the sea, a whole summer away, and Lenu can't think of anything but the guilt she feels in leaving Lila to fend for herself against her father, her brother, and the beautiful, controlling Marcello who has come for her. She can't kill them all, and the knowledge is like dying. Lenu has been offered an exit, and what does Lila say? She says, "Brava." She says, "Go into the world for the two of us." The thing is, it's impossible to feel joy if you are the female who has gotten away and you know it's a fluke, and it doesn't change the condition of the others.

December 4, 2018. *My Brilliant Friend,* Episode 6. As soon as we see the mustache twitching, we know Lenu is in the line of its fire. Lila's father's sale of her to a beautiful man is a homoerotic exchange. The father is jonesing for this man from the moment the young man steps into his world. Maybe every exchange of this kind is two men fucking through the proxy of the girl. Maybe all male supremacy is men fucking each other in various ways.

The question of males' feelings about themselves as men is a blob that keeps expanding, no matter what Lila does to fend it off. You run, and you run, and there it is. If you are a male human, and you are not able to enter the story of these two girls as if the story is about you, then you are the ball in the Indiana Jones movies coming to crush them. This show is saying this in every shot. It is so beautiful and sad. Go, Lenu, ride those waves, read those books, stroke through that water, go get your friend, cry your eyes out, stay alive.

December 12, 2018. *My Brilliant Friend,* Episodes 7 and 8. The show is interested only in the relationship between the girls. All the other characters are instrumental to this unfolding engagement. There is no other interiority but theirs and only a dawning interiority for Lila.

The first season is done. Episode 7 was a bit of a slog. Too much boy and not enough Lenu and Lila. Each girl picks a less violent male she doesn't desire to fend off a more violent male who arouses rage. In the case of Lila and Marcello, the beautiful, rich-boy bully, it's more than rage. It's also sexual attraction. Who has not hated a person you also wanted to fuck? She tells him she will kill him if he replaces her with another attraction. At the same time, she agrees to marry her smitten boy if he promises to keep Marcello away from her. She doesn't want to be in Marcello's power. It would be worse than being in the power of her father and brother, who are dominating but at least afraid of her.

Lenu lets a boy feel her up because she can use him to scare off the twitching mustache letch who molested her the summer before and whose son she wants. It's confusing. It's all confusing. The less violent males turn out to have their own agendas, and they are not really less violent, only more smitten and temporarily malleable.

It's enjoyable and painful to see Lenu in love with the letch's son, a surly, baby intellectual with unshaven fuzz. Her eyes grow soft and hazy. Impulsively she presses his hand to the table, wanting him to stay at the wedding party, even after he's rejected a piece she's written for his little journal. She has been burning to see her name in print. The boy has been told Lenu is a better writer than him, and the piece has been polished by Lila so it reflects a combination of their abilities. Lenu is disappointed. You can see the light go out of her eyes and the air leave her chest, but when you want someone, what's one more piece of power you let them have over you? He still walks out.

In Episode 8, the season finale, Lila and Lenu are back together, and we see what we have seen from their first moments together: each for the other is the only person in the world who speaks their language. Not to share a language is isolation of a deranging sort. To share a language is to share an inner and outer world of understandings.

To the girls, the phrase, "normal life" translates into, "male control that will block all exits or produce so much trauma the exits won't be visible." Lila decides to go entirely underground, where she has mostly lived with the exception of Lenu's friendship, and marry a man she does not love in order to leave the home of her father and brother. In this calculation, Lila sees what she is turning into.

Lenu comes to see it, too. It's spoken of by the girls in their funny, truncated bursts of dialogue and sudden avowals of belief in each other. The scene of Lenu bathing Lila before her fake happy wedding is breathtaking. "Stand up," Lenu says to Lila, and she rises, naked, and we see the glory of youth's body she is going to trade away. The mind that has devised the trade puts at risk the cascade of language in her, depositing more and more along a restless shore. The teacher who discovered the genius in the little girl thinks Lila's great gifts have been scattered and swept away. She won't allow her into her apartment.

December 20, 2018. Now that my sister is dead, I see my mother in the mirror. She liked to talk to strangers. She was funny and mean, and I miss my sister, who loved her.

PERSONAL LIFE

On the romance of being number 2 and other attachments

Catherine Millet posed naked for her husband, Jacques Henric, beginning in 1972, during the decades she was editor of *ArtPress*, the influential Paris journal she co-founded. In some of the photographs, her legs are spread, and you can make out the faint line where the lips of her vulva meet. She looks like someone who has opened a closet and found herself accidentally onstage. She bows her head as if her head is an incumbrance.

*

On a cold night in 1957, Jack Kerouac, 35, phoned Joyce Glassman, 21, and asked if they could meet. Allen Ginsberg had given Kerouac her number. Jack's last girlfriend had thrown him out, calling him a paranoid, womanizing drunk. He was broke, and it would be nine months before *On the Road* would make him famous. Joyce went to meet him at a Howard Johnson and paid for his hot dog and beans. When he asked to spend the night she said of course.

*

Susanna Kaysen developed a pain in her vagina and chronicled the experience in *The Camera My Mother Gave Me*. She was in her late 40s when the pain began with the insistence of toothache that felt sharpest when she drove wearing pants. Attempts at sex made her vagina feel scraped by a cheese grater. She tried estrogen cream, Novocain cream, and cortisone. She bathed in boric acid and tea. She was treated for yeast infections and the consequences of treating yeast infections. She took an antidepressant that made her moronic. She tried biofeedback, where she was coached to pee less frequently. She kept a "pain diary," visited a vulvologist, and developed her pelvic floor muscles.

She read literature published by the National Vulvodynia and Vestibulitis Association. She read the *Clinical Journal of Pain* and *Obstetrics and Gynecology*. A surgeon said he could cut a hole in her vagina to fix it, but the healing could last as long as two and half months, during which time the vagina is "basically an open wound." In addition, the procedure failed to benefit 55 percent of those who tried it.

During the years Kaysen was in pain, her boyfriend pressed her for intercourse, even though she offered alternative kinds of sex. Friends advised her to cut him loose. She did not.

*

In 1851, Elizabeth Siddal posed for "Ophelia," the famous painting by John Everett Millais, lying in a tub of water in a long white dress. The tub was supposed to be heated by oil lamps, but Millais, in the throes of creation, forgot about his model and let the lamps die down. He realized she was freezing by the chatter of her teeth. In 1862, at age 30, Siddal died of an overdose of laudanum. In *The Lives of the Muses* (2003), Francine Prose commended Siddal for dying young, judging her writing maudlin and her paintings unrealized.

*

The movie *Henry & June* (1990, directed by Philip Kaufman) is based on the diaries of Anaïs Nin, in which Nin chronicles her affairs with Henry Miller and Miller's flamboyant wife June. The setting is Paris in the 1920s, where Nin ventures into *la vie bohème*, believing she is going out on a limb. In the movie, when she feels threatened or sad, she retreats to her husband, Hugo, who is rich and calls her "pussy-willow." In the diaries that Nin published, Hugo is not mentioned.

In the movie's last scene, the Nin character weeps, looking out the window of a car as Henry rides behind her on a bicycle. She claims she is grieving for the end of their affair, but you don't think that is why she is crying. You think she is crying because Henry is a better writer than she is, and he is a better writer because he lives without a safety net.

*

Gustave Flaubert and the writer Louise Colet had been lovers for several months when he wrote to her: "People in love can go for years without seeing each other." Another time he wrote: "Women mistake their cunt for their heart and think the moon is made to illuminate their boudoir." He wrote: "Why do you always take the defense [of the female sex]? One must always be on the side of the strong." He wrote: "When has a woman ever died of rape?" And in one of his final letters to Colet, written in 1854, he wrote: "I've always tried (but it seems I've failed) to turn you into a sublime hermaphrodite. . . I would wish you to be a man from the waist up. Going downward you encumber me and trouble me and damage me with your femaleness."

*

The artist Lee Krasner (b. 1908) was the daughter of Russian-Jewish immigrants, who spoke with a blunt, adenoidal bark. She fought her way into Washington Irving High School, the only public school where she could major in art, and later attended Cooper Union and the National Academy of Design. Starting in 1934, she supported herself with commissions from the WPA. From 1937 to 1940, she studied with Hans Hofmann, who introduced her to improvisation and guided her shift from realism to abstraction. She was 33 in 1941 when she met Jackson Pollock. At the time, she was covering canvases with a riot of markings and Hofmann said of her work, "This is so good, you wouldn't know it was painted by a woman." When she moved into Pollock's apartment, she arranged for the art patron Peggy Guggenheim to see their work. Guggenheim first darted into the room where Krasner painted and huffed, "I didn't come all this way to see LK." LK is the way Krasner signed her canvases.

*

In 2000, Joyce Johnson published *Door Wide Open: Jack Kerouac & Joyce Johnson, A Beat Love Affair in Letters, 1957-1958*. In Kerouac's letters to Johnson, he fears for his work after Ginsberg's poem *Howl* is tried for obscenity. He refers to his books as "great," compares himself to Shakespeare, and declares a play he is writing will be "the funniest comedy in the history of American theater." In other letters, he lists chores for Johnson to perform, referring to her as "my little secretary."

She writes to him about hearing Coltrane for the first time, discovering the Lower East Side, meeting painter Franz Kline and photographer Robert Frank. She secures a contract with Random House for her first novel, *Come and Join the Dance,* which is published when she is 26. During the year and ten months she corresponded with Kerouac, he traveled to Tangiers and as she was arranging to join him, he decamped for California. When she made plans to fly to see him in California, he took off for Mexico. She addressed him as "sweetie" and "baby" and said she understood his changes of plans.

In notes Johnson includes with the letters, she describes a visit to Kerouac when he was living with his mother in Northport, Long Island. Johnson has begged to come there, and he has not been able to say no. He does not meet her at the station and is drunk by the time she arrives at the house. Later that day, young girls drive up and sweep him off to a party she is not invited to. Months later, at a dinner party, he flirts with a woman in front of her, and Johnson walks away for the last time. Seeing her leave, he calls out, "Unrequited love's a bore." Johnson says in her notes: "It would be a mistake for the reader to put too much emphasis upon what Jack Kerouac withheld from me and to forget what he'd had to give. He'd written to a very young woman as an equal, someone strong enough to take the truth." She continues, "He could behave unforgivably, yet you would ultimately have to forgive him." She doesn't say why.

*

Sylvia Plath met Ted Hughes in 1956, during a year she spent in Cambridge on a Fulbright. The poets were introduced at a party in February and were married in June. Between these dates, another boyfriend of Plath's skipped out of a rendezvous with her in Paris. After Hughes and Plath became a couple, she typed his poems and sent them to publishers. In her diary and letters, she describes him as a god she wants to put first. They split up in 1962 after Hughes began an affair with Assia Wevill. (After seven years with Hughes, Assia, too, gassed herself and their little girl.) At the time of Plath's death in 1963, Hughes was an acclaimed poet. *Ariel*, the collection of poems that would cement her reputation, appeared posthumously. On the brink of suicide, she was contending with a husband in love with another woman. Her writing was prompting lukewarm reviews. She was caring for two small children. And she was looking out at the prospect of a frigid, London winter. In *The Savage God*, Plath's friend A. Alvarez argues that she wanted to be discovered and saved.

*

In *The Audition* (1989), a short film by Anna Campion, the sister of Jane Campion, two actresses play Jane and the sisters' mother. The mother once aspired to act, so Jane casts her in a small role in a movie she is directing. In front of the camera, the mother is nervous and flubs her lines. Once she relaxes, though, she's brilliant. When the mother is praised, she insists she's been pressured to perform. She recalls a retreat where she and Jane practiced "embracing their power." Looking out with annoyance, she says, "I never wanted to own my own life."

Early one morning the mother rouses Jane and asks if she ever feels anxious and despairing. Jane describes a calming technique she practices, and her mother cuts her off, looking fretfully about the room before settling on Jane, and saying, "We should have had that mole removed long ago." When Jane is typing at a window, her mother sets a lawn sprinkler to beat against the glass. Jane readies herself for a bike ride, and her mother warns her of the dangers of the road. Later, in her car, she breezes past a rain-soaked Jane, stopped at the side of the road. At the prospect of weekend guests, the mother says, "I'm tired of shopping and cooking." Jane says, "Don't be a food martyr, Mom," suggesting that guests contribute pot-luck style. The mother says, "Oh, Jane, you don't care about other people."

*

Michael Haneke's film *The Piano Teacher* (2001) is based on the novel by Austrian writer Elfriede Jelinek, who won a Nobel Prize in 2004. Isabelle Huppert plays the title character, named Erika Kohut, with the impassive mask of a sleepwalker. She is in her 40s and lives with her mother in Vienna, where she teaches at the premier music conservatory. Mother and daughter sleep in the same bed. One day Erika arrives home from school, wearing her customary white shirt and dark skirt and her hair secured with clasps. Swiftly, she locks the bathroom door, removes a razor from her purse, hoists up her skirt, and cuts her vagina, shutting her eyes and shuddering. Blood drips into the tub. She swishes it down the drain and slips a sanitary pad into her panties. She wears a bathrobe to dinner, and her mother sits across from her, watching TV. When the mother notices a red stream trickling down her daughter's leg, she points and twists her mouth in disgust.

*

Simone de Beauvoir was the youngest and most brilliant *agrégé* in the history of French education for women. In 1929, she placed first in her final exams at the Sorbonne but was given a second prize because Jean-Paul Sartre was male and had failed the year before.

*

In the 1950s and early 1960s, four female movie stars loomed above the rest: Elizabeth Taylor, Marilyn Monroe, Doris Day, and Audrey Hepburn. Taylor and Monroe were sexual, Day and Hepburn were virgins. Taylor's beauty was represented as a force subsuming even her own will. Monroe was the girl who is poor and desperate enough to dance at a stag party. Day was the small-town blonde whose anxiety about sex was projected as virtue. Long-legged Hepburn, who lacked hips and a bust, cut an androgynous figure. Her neck was swanlike, her eyes large and liquid.

The figure Hepburn projected was sprightly, gamine, poised, well-bred. Her diction was a flurry of clipped, bright sounds, punctuated with slow, drawn-out effects. Her smile was adorable. In adversity she was resolute. Hollywood paired her with fathers. In *Sabrina* (1954), she ends up with Humphrey Bogart. In *Love in the Afternoon* (1957), made when she was 27, she is paired with an exhausted-looking Gary Cooper, who was 57 at the time. In 1963, she played opposite Cary Grant and the next year against Rex Harrison in *My Fair Lady*. In *Funny Face*, also made in 1957, she teamed with Fred Astaire, who was 30 years her senior.

During the filming of *Funny Face*, her weight slipped below 100 pounds. In the 1950s and early 1960s, people did not speak about radical dieting. No one mentioned that Audrey Hepburn dieted or that her British banker father, Joseph Anthony Hepburn-Ruston, was an early advocate of Hitler and served as an officer in Oswald Mosley's Black Shirt Brigade. She adored him.

Her mother was critical of her body and choices in men. Hepburn had been a chubby child and adolescent, fattening on chocolates and other sweets. After she slimmed, she would binge on puddings, éclairs, boxes of candy. In 1961, Hal Wallis considered casting her in *Summer and Smoke* but decided against it when she insisted Givenchy design clothes for the drab schoolteacher she was cast to play. The same year, in *The Children's Hour*, Hepburn played a teacher falsely accused of lesbianism. She worried her association with lesbianism, even in a movie, would mar her image. The image she wished to carve was the absence of struggle.

*

In 1884, Camille Claudel began an affair with Auguste Rodin, who was twice her age and had been involved for twenty years with Rose

Beuret, with whom he had a child. For nine years Rodin was also Claudel's lover. She worked on some of his most celebrated commissions as well as on pieces of her own. She became pregnant and did not tell him, asking him to choose her over Rose. When he refused to decide, she had an abortion, withheld the information, and rented a workshop of her own.

Claudel and Rodin continued on and off for another five years. The pieces she sculpted depicted threat, regret, and abandonment. She retreated from the world. When the Seine flooded her workshop, she did not rouse herself to escape. In time, she boarded up her windows and left her studio only at night. Still, Rodin tried to secure commissions for her. At the opening of an exhibition of her work, organized by her bronze caster and friend Eugene Blot, she showed up drunk, bleary-eyed, and disheveled. In 1914, her mother, with whom she'd battled, committed her to a mental institution, where she lived until her death in 1943. At the institution, she would eat only raw eggs and potatoes in their skins, believing she was being poisoned.

*

In 1938, Jean-Paul Sartre wrote to Simone de Beauvoir, his lover, about his latest affair: "A day of passion disturbed around noon when I gave Tania a playful tap on the behind. She made a fuss: I blew up the whole incident; she sobbed; I was wretched. The balance sheet is as follows. It is understood that I am a master manipulator, there's even talk of blows and kisses mixed. She doesn't try to hide the pleasure she gets out of it... I'm used to easier women... But ultimately, of all those who have honored me with their ardor these past few months, there's not one who's been so pleasing physically and so moving in the realm of passion."

*

In *Jane Eyre*, after Bertha Mason burns down Thornfield Hall, Edward Rochester lives in Ferndean, a smaller house on his estate. Still raven-haired and virile looking, he is blind, missing a hand, and God-fearing—believing now that God has punished him for proposing to Jane while still married to Bertha. Early in the novel, Jane stands atop Thornfield Hall and gazes at far-off towns, conjuring a vision of travel and like-minded travelers. Charlotte Brontë was imagining the life she would one day lead in London as a famous author. Jane abandons this ambition for a life with Rochester she calls "a marriage of equals." To create this union, Brontë joins a physically dependent man (although Rochester will recover his sight in time) and an economically independent woman. (Jane has returned newly rich with an inheritance from a dead uncle.) She slips into the role of caretaker, an occupation that does not bore her or threaten her life, tending, as she puts it, "this royal eagle, chained to a perch." To the reader, she confides, "He saw nature—he saw books through me." For the woman to serve, the man must be a wreck.

*

Robert Lowell was nicknamed Cal in boarding school, short for "Caligula" and sometimes "Caliban." Before he began taking lithium in the early 1970s, he imagined he was Alexander the Great and Napoleon, as well as modern tyrants such as Hitler. He once held Allen Tate outside an open window while reciting one of Tate's poems. He slapped his first wife, the novelist Jean Stafford, so hard he rebroke the nose that had shattered when he drove their car into a wall. In 1980, Lowell's friend Frank Parker told Lowell biographer Ian Hamilton, "Mind you, we none of us ever thought Cal was crazy or anything. He was just a violent man doing his own thing." In 1947, Stafford wrote to Lowell, "What do I care if Randall [Jarrell] likes my books? Or anyone? Why should it console me to be praised as a good writer? . . . There is nothing worse for a woman than to be deprived of her womanliness. For me, there is nothing worse than the knowledge that life holds nothing for me but being a writer."

*

In 1948, RDR (Rassemblement Démocratique Révolutionnaire), the radical political organization in which Sartre and de Beauvoir were active, invited de Beauvoir to speak at an assembly. RDR extended an invitation as well to Richard Wright, wishing to redress the exclusion of women and blacks from positions of prominence in the organization. Albert Camus, who did not want to watch a woman address a room of men, successfully lobbied to remove de Beauvoir from the roster. She was permitted to appear only as Wright's translator. She agreed to the arrangement. Sartre did not protest on her behalf, and she said she did not expect him to.

*

In an early scene in the movie *Pollock* (2000), Marcia Gay Harden, playing Lee Krasner, stands in a doorway. It's the day Pollock has come to her studio and said, "You're damned good for a woman painter." She invites him out for coffee. They sit in a café, and we see Harden-Krasner several times restrain herself from touching his hand. Ed Harris, who also directed, plays Pollock not in the taciturn, aloof-but-crackling style of Gary Cooper or Clint Eastwood. His Pollock emits a radical passivity, a crashing nothing. Yet Harden-Krasner is undeterred, seeing in him something familiar. He looks at her the way the world looks at her.

Back at her apartment, she doesn't turn on the lights, and there is no conversation. She is exhausted from trying to extract something from this man. There is a long hallway; at one end is her bedroom and at the other end is her studio. Harris-Pollock stands as far from the bedroom as possible. Maybe he's afraid he won't be able to perform, given his drinking. Harden-Krasner walks toward the bedroom, peeling off clothes, less in the manner of a seducer than a farmhand facing chores. The camera feels for her unloved flesh, and it shows her becoming both people as she speaks for the man in her head. Harris-Pollock watches Harden-Krasner remove her blouse and bra and free her large breasts in the frame of the door. She waits. At last he moves forward, an animal trudging toward the barn, and it is to a barn she will eventually lead him, where, in East Hampton, he will produce his masterpieces.

*

De Beauvoir put aside writing *The Second Sex* to prepare a screenplay of Sartre's *Dirty Hands*. (He was paying her). When she was writing *The Mandarins*, she devoted sixteen-hour days to Sartre's 800-page manuscript on Genet. He read her glancingly, if at all. After *The Second Sex* was published and a consensus formed, joined by Sartre, that Beauvoir's book would influence society more than any of Sartre's works, she maintained that her contribution to society would be measured by her role in Sartre's life. She published the letters he had written to her, detailing his many affairs with other women, in order to prove her centrality in his intellectual development. She told Deirdre Bair, who was writing a biography of her, "Anyone who reads his letters to me will know what I meant to him."

*

In 1958, after another of Lowell's affairs and breakdowns, Elizabeth Hardwick, to whom he was married, wrote to a cousin of Lowell's: "These damned girls complicate everything; they keep me from acting in his best interests often because I don't want to seem pushing or jealous."

In 1961, Hardwick wrote to Lowell, who was planning to return to her after an affair with the poet Sandra Hochman: "I hope you won't become so vexed with the horrors of settling into your new life that you'll want to flee it. By the way, do you think you would be happier with a little apartment of your own? ... I really want to make the effort to give you—or allow you—the life that is most healthy for you and am going to make a really superhuman effort to improve as a wife so that your home and daily life won't make you sick again."

In 1965, following Lowell's affair with an actress named Vija Vetra, Hardwick wrote to her husband: "Cal, my heart bleeds for you, but remember what greatness you have made of your life, what joy you have given to all of us. My purpose, beloved, is to try to see *what can be done to help us all*. I hate for you to get sick. I would kill myself, if it would cure you. There must be something more we can lean on—medical, psychiatric, personal, the dearest love goes out to you from your apartment here on 67th Street. I long to talk to you again."

*

In 1959, Susan Sontag, then 26, wrote in her journal, "My desire to write is connected with my homosexuality. I need the identity [of writer] as a weapon, to match the weapon that society has against me. It doesn't justify my homosexuality. But it would give me—I feel—a license. I am just becoming aware of how guilty I feel being queer."

*

In October 2003, Timothy Treadwell was eaten by a bear in Katmai, Alaska. Before his death, he had viewed the ferocity of grizzlies as a form of neurosis, produced by human fear of them. He aimed to prove this by showing the gentle way grizzlies treated him. In footage he shot of himself, he cuts a childish, theatrical figure with a blonde, Prince Valiant hairdo tucked beneath a bandana. He nicknamed the bears Thumper, Hulk, Mr. Chocolate, Squiggle, Czar and Booble. For thirteen summers, starting in 1990, Treadwell got down on all fours, sang and read to the bears.

In October 2003, he and his girlfriend, Amie Huguenard, who was afraid of bears, were attacked and dismembered by a mean grizzly not known to Treadwell. They had returned to camp later than usual and at a time, before hibernating, when bears feed aggressively. Had someone other than Treadwell met this end, it would have made gory tabloid copy, but it would not have inspired Werner Herzog to make a film, nor would a Treadwell who had gone on mingling with bears unharmed. It is the combination of hubris and Treadwell's comeuppance that serves Herzog and makes *Grizzly Man*, released in 2005, difficult to watch.

*

In *Seduction and Betrayal* (1974), Elizabeth Hardwick extols the character of Thea in *Hedda Gabler*: "One of those opportunities for transcendence suddenly changed Thea's nothingness to the most joyful promise. She meets Eilert Løvborg... a thinker, an artist, a bohemian, a sort of Nietzschean figure whose career and accomplishments have been spoiled by drinking. Thea falls in love with him. But it is more than romance; it is a mission, a sacred trust, one of those dedications that challenge the very essence of a superior woman. Løvborg is more than a romantic man; he is the instrument through which Thea can find some purpose for her own intellectual possibilities. She is a sort of graduate student; she believes in learning, in writing, in art, in culture. The flames of a passionate collaboration consume her. To live with Løvborg, keep him from drinking, help him to bring into actual being the books he has wanted to write, this mission absorbs her whole heart."

*

In *The Lives of the Muses* (2002), Francine Prose proposes that women cannot take men as muses. Men, she says, see a woman as a featureless abstraction and a surface on which to project their ideas. Women, she says, in order to insure the survival of the species, "are trained to pay close attention to the particular needs, the specific qualities of an *individual* man." Women, she says, create to seduce. Men, according to Prose, create to please themselves. Men become excited by beautiful females, but they do not aim their work to win them, she says. She makes scant mention of same-sex couples but allows Alice B. Toklas as a muse for Gertrude Stein. Prose doesn't comment on male muses of men, say Bosie to Oscar Wilde.

*

In 1949, New York School painters founded the Eighth Street Club to talk with art critics and curators about avant-garde work. Women were mostly admitted into the audience, and even those accepted as members—Lee Krasner among them—weren't included on the board or in policy discussions. In 1949, Sidney Janis organized the group show "Man and Wife." Women were invited to show only within the category "wife." Krasner participated. After withering reviews of her work, she did not show again until 1951.

From 1945 to 1956, when Krasner lived with Pollock in East Hampton, she painted in a small bedroom, working on a series of "little image" paintings. Mostly they measured 24' by 30' and were filled with beautiful, repeating forms that look like hieroglyphs. She did not display this work in 1951 at her first one-woman show at the Betty Parsons Gallery. Parsons was Pollock's dealer. Pollock urged Parsons to show Krasner, but when he left the gallery, Parsons severed her connection with Krasner.

Krasner's tendency during this time was to cut up her paintings or rub off images until almost none of the original paint was left. She showed again in 1955 at Eleanor Ward's Stable Gallery, mounting big collage works she created from her cut-up paintings, pieces of Pollock's discarded canvases, and black paper. Clement Greenberg highly praised the show.

*

In *The Philosophy of Andy Warhol: (From A to B and Back Again),* Warhol writes of being shot by Valerie Solanas: "Before I was shot I always thought that I was more half-there than all-there—I always suspected that I was watching TV instead of living life. People sometimes say that the way things happen in movies is unreal, but actually it's the way things happen in life that's unreal. The movies make emotions look so strong and real, whereas when things really do happen to you, it's like watching television—you don't feel anything. Right when I was being shot and ever since, I knew that I was watching television. The channels switch, but it's all television."

*

In *Seduction and Betrayal,* Hardwick writes of Hedda Gabler: "Her determination to destroy the worthy, loving, serious Thea, if for no reason or gain to herself, comes from a nature not only damaged but fundamentally low... It is Iago's destructive compulsion, rooted at one moment in a triviality, and at another in something more threatening but never adequate to the destroying impulses. There is waywardness in her never to be explained..."

But Ibsen does explain it. It is the impetus of his play. To him, Hedda has reached a dead end in the possibilities for nineteenth century women. She does not appreciate Thea's devotion to Løvborg because she does not want to help Løvborg. She wants to be Løvborg. Knowing she cannot because she is uneducated and enfeebled in other ways, she turns violent. To see Hedda's predicament, you have to sympathize with her refusal to play the roles of wife and disciple. Hedda is smart enough to know what has been denied to her and too weak to change the world.

*

The mauling of Timothy Treadwell is at the center of Werner Herzog's interest in him, and he uses Treadwell as a cautionary tale about the perils of projecting human understandings onto nature. It does not occur to him that his view, too, is a human understanding. Maybe nature is not always indifferent. The bear that attacked Treadwell was a stranger while none of the bears he interacted with regularly harmed him. Maybe they didn't want to. To Herzog, indifferent nature is something a man can look up to. Indifferent nature is the quintessence of macho. Herzog's view of Treadwell is a version of the bullying he sought to escape by toughening his body and living apart from human beings in the wilderness. If we don't regard Treadwell's loneliness, what are we looking at?

*

At 42, ill with breast cancer, Susan Sontag wrote in her journal, "I feel my body has let me down. And my mind, too. For, somewhere, I believe the Reichian verdict. I'm responsible for my cancer. I lived as a coward, repressing my desire, my rage."

*

Recognition for the work of American women artists in the first half of the twentieth century—among them Elaine de Kooning, Dorothy Dehner, Grace Hartigan, Helen Frankenthaler, Joan Mitchell, Louise Nevelson, and Lee Krasner—was deferred far longer than for their male contemporaries, some of whom were their mates. Dehner didn't start sculpting professionally until, at nearly 50, she left her husband, sculptor David Smith.

Women painters were not drinking in the Cedar Bar because women painters weren't welcome there. Interviewed about the bar scene years later, Krasner said women were "treated like cattle." After 1956, when Pollock drunkenly plowed his car into a tree, killing himself and one of his female passengers, Krasner produced new paintings, some abstract, some including figures, and created an important body of large collages. She had learned from Pollock but did not adopt his style, continuing to feel kinship with Matisse and Mondrian. In 1973, the Whitney produced a show of her work, and in 1984, the year she died of internal bleeding from diverticulitis, the Museum of Modern Art exhibited the first full retrospective of her work in the United States.

*

George Balanchine preferred not to see the women he had loved in his youth. He didn't want their aged faces and bodies to color his memories. He was 40 years older than seventeen-year-old Suzanne Farrell when she joined his company in 1961. In 1969, he fired her for declining to sleep with him and for marrying another dancer. After a separation of seven years, Balanchine took her back. They did not discuss what had happened.

*

In 2005, Toni Bentley, a former dancer with New York City Ballet, published *The Surrender: An Erotic Memoir,* in which she reports having anal intercourse over three years a total of 298 times. Little about her lover is revealed other than that his penis is large and he enjoys the challenge of her tight, boy-sized parts. When Bentley and her lover are together, he enters her three times a week with full, ramming penetration that extends for hours. The activity, she says, releases her pelvic floor muscles, screwed closed from years at the barre. She saves her lover's used condoms in a special little box. "Anal sex," she writes, "is about cooperation. Cooperation in an endeavor of aristocratic politics, involving rigid hierarchies, feudal positions, and monarchist attitudes. One is in charge, the other obedient. Entirely in charge. Entirely obedient."

*

In a nude photograph of Catherine Millet, shot by her husband, she is on her hands and knees, and a man's boot is pressed against her ass. Her ass is round and shapely. The picture is cropped so all you see of the man is his leg and upper body, clothed in the garb of a military officer.

*

In 1991, Anita Hill passed a lie detector test before testifying against the fitness of Clarence Thomas to serve on the US Supreme Court. Thomas refused to take a polygraph test. For two years, when Hill worked as Thomas's assistant at the US Department of Education and the Equal Employment Opportunity Commission, he repeatedly asked her out socially and refused to take no for an answer. She said he spoke to her about "women having sex with animals and films showing group sex or rape scenes." On several occasions, he graphically described "his own sexual prowess" and details of his anatomy. She famously recounted an instance in which he examined a can of Coke on his desk and asked, "Who has put pubic hair on my Coke?"

Four female witnesses, waiting in the wings to support Hill's credibility, were not called because, according to the *Los Angeles Times*, the Senate Judiciary Committee chair, Joe Biden, struck a deal with "aggressive, gloves-off Republicans." In televised hearings, the country watched Thomas call Hill a liar, a fantasist, and a fanatic. He lumped the women's movement with establishment racism by accusing feminists of targeting an innocent black man. He made these statements although he and Hill, two people of color, discredited affirmative action and eroded protection from bias for people of color while working at the EEOC. In 1991, when women were polled about who they believed, the majority said Thomas was telling the truth.

*

In *The Virgin Suicides* (1993), Jeffrey Eugenides creates a collective narrator of middle-aged men who contemplate five sisters who have killed themselves. The men pore over photographs, eyewitness accounts, and the sisters' diaries, claiming a sense of identification with them: "We felt the imprisonment of being a girl, the way it made your mind active and dreamy, and you ended up knowing which colors went together." Jonathan Swift wrote poems depicting Stella defecating and farting. Eugenides's narrator inventories the suffering of the girls and catalogues their real and imagined odors, comparing "trapped beaver" to the dead-fish flies that plague the suburban neighborhood where the novel is set. The girls' bodies are compared to "bad breath, cheese, milk, tongue film, . . . [and] the singed smell of drilled teeth." The smells of male bodies are not noted.

*

In the late 1960s and early 1970s, as the women's movement built momentum, some women in Lee Krasner's generation wondered about the choices they had made. Some felt attacked and defended themselves. In 1970, Krasner joined a picket of the Museum of Modern Art for neglecting women artists but did not identify herself as a feminist. When asked why she didn't promote her work the way she did her husband's, she told the interviewer, "I couldn't run out and do a one-woman job on the sexist aspects of the art world, continue my painting, and stay in the role I was in as Mrs. Pollock. I just couldn't do that much. What I considered important was that I was able to work and other things would have to take their turn. Now rightly or wrongly, I made my decisions."

*

In an interview, Alfred Kazin told Francis Kiernan, who was researching a biography of Mary McCarthy, that he didn't find McCarthy sexy because (a) she "was a little too clever and talkative" and (b) she had "a hearty, Irish laugh, a nervous laugh."

*

In the novel *Smell* (1999), by Radhika Jha, the mother of an Indian girl sends her daughter to live in Paris. There, the girl develops a preternatural sense of smell. She can sniff out character in a person through the scents they give off. After a string of bad boyfriends, she comes to believe her body reeks, and no evidence to the contrary can dissuade her.

*

Writing in her journal, Susan Sontag invented the term "X" for times she protected herself: "'X' is when you . . . want to please and impress people, either by saying what they want to hear, or by shocking them, or by boasting and name dropping or by being very cool."

*

In *The Sexual Life of Catherine M.*, Catherine Millet describes having sex with thousands of men and some women in scores of settings between the late 1960s and 2002, the time of publication. Routinely she had sex with 40 men in a single gang-bang or mingled with more than that number as part of an undulating orgy blob. She had quick and sudden sex in the Bois de Boulogne, on roadsides and at truck stops, in apartments, in her dentist's office, and in the closet of her office at *ArtPress*. Almost nightly and with the knowledge of her husband, she attended freeform parties, known in France as *partouzes*.

She liked being handed off to men by other men, surrendering her will to anyone willing to steer it. She liked being submerged in a communal heap of bodies where her face wasn't distinct, and she connects this penchant with being Catholic, which she jettisoned at seventeen when she began having sex. Feeling shy and plain, sex became a way of being with people, including people in the art world with whom she would make her life. In response to a reporter's question about why she wrote the memoir, she said, "Because it was missing."

*

In *The Piano Teacher*, Erika dons a little scarf between lessons and visits sex shops, where she watches violent videos. At a drive-in, she peers into a window and observes a man enter a woman. When the woman cries out at climax, Erika squats beside the car and quietly urinates, her eyes squeezed tight. When the man opens the car and calls out, "pervert," she scurries off with an inscrutable expression.

At night in bed, she throws herself on top of her mother, pins her hands, and kisses her mouth, crying out, "I love you." A brash, beautiful seventeen-year-old named Walter becomes her student. At first she belittles him. After they go to bed, she writes out instructions, asking to be tied up and beaten. He says he loves her and is repulsed by her conditions. She becomes enraged and jealous of other girls he sees. Fed up with her theatrics, he charges up to her apartment, shoves aside her mother, locks the door of her room, and beats and rapes her. "Is this what you want, what you've imagined?" he shouts. Sprawled on the floor with a bloody lip, Erika shakes her head no.

*

Gordon (1966), by Edith Templeton, chronicles a nine-month, sadomasochistic affair the author had in London with a Scottish psychiatrist she calls Richard Gordon. The affair, she told the *New York Times*, was "the fundamental event" of her life. The narrator, called Louisa, is 28 and living in a bedsitter when Gordon picks her up in a pub, whisks her to a decrepit garden, and within an hour rams himself into her without speaking. She likes it and she doesn't like it, and it is this rupture from the rational that hooks her.

She doesn't ask the reader to love Gordon. She reveals he's skinny, takes forever to come, can have sex only when she is on her back, unmoving, and he becomes enraged by the rejection of women.

Gordon determines when she may pee. He rapes her outdoors in a rundown part of Soho and takes her to a party, her clothes shredded and her bruises visible. Sitting at his feet as commanded, she surveys the damage, noticing "patches of greenish slime" on her skirt that "might have been traces of putrid vegetables." When the hostess asks in an anxious whisper if she's okay, Louisa says to the reader, "I thought with derision how benighted she was, and that it was just because Gordon had mortified me and shown that he owned me that I was happy... I felt free to behave as badly as I wanted to."

*

In Two Lives: Gertrude and Alice (2008), Janet Malcolm commends Gertrude Stein for detaching language from lockstep syntax and narrative determinacy. Malcolm enjoys the way Stein celebrates herself, especially in *The Autobiography of Alice B. Toklas,* where Malcolm says Stein subverted autobiography by "dispensing with the fiction of humility" and rejecting "the flaccid narrativity of biography" in favor of "the bracing storylessness of human life."

*

In *The Second Sex,* published in 1949, de Beauvoir writes, "It must be admitted that the males find in women more complicity than the oppressor usually finds in the oppressed. And in bad faith they take authorization from this to declare that she has *desired* the destiny they have imposed on her. We have seen that all the main features of her training combine to bar her from the roads of revolt and adventure. Society in general—beginning with her respected parents—lies to her by praising the lofty values of love, devotion, the gift of herself, and then concealing from her the fact that neither her lover nor husband nor yet her children will be inclined to accept the burdensome charge of all that. She cheerfully believes these lies because they invite her to follow the easy slope. In this others commit the worst crime against her: Throughout her life from childhood on, they damage and corrupt her by designating as her true vocation this submission, which is the temptation of every existent in the anxiety of liberty."

*

Charlotte Brontë's publisher said she would have traded all her genius to be beautiful. The novelist Dawn Powell wrote in her diary, "For a genius to be a genius, he must have a selfless slave between himself and the world." In *Story of O,* O strives to be the best submissive in the chateau and winds up in a corner, wearing an owl mask. Stendhal wrote, "All of us would prefer to spend our lives with a woman servant than a woman savant." In the monologue *It's a Slippery Slope* (1996), Spalding Gray says he chose neither his longtime girlfriend Renée nor Kathie, the woman who gave birth to his child, but rather the mirror of himself he saw in the little boy: "There is always another woman, but never another son." During the fourteen years Lee Krasner and Jackson Pollock were married, Pollock rose from obscurity to widespread confirmation that his spatter paintings were works of genius; Krasner shifted from centering her life around her art to devoting herself to her husband's career. In *Wuthering Heights*, Heathcliff and Cathy do not work, marry, or have sex. They are outlaw lovers, in revolt against the social world where sex and class do, in fact, defeat them. In a diary entry of 1958, Susan Sontag wrote, "One of the main (social) functions of a journal or diary is precisely to be read furtively by... the people (like parents + lovers) about whom one has been cruelly honest only in the journal." In *The Second Sex*, de Beauvoir assumes that socialist revolution will end sexual inequality, even though Sartre, a leftist, thought men could do as they pleased and women could not. De Beauvoir believed that economic independence would lift the pressure on women to play traditional roles, even though having money did not render her emotionally free.

*

In a profile of Roman Polanski, Lawrence Weschsler remarks on the pile-up of horror in the director's life. He is referring to Polanski's Holocaust childhood during which his mother was killed, to the murder of Sharon Tate by Charles Manson's gang, and to Polanski's arrest for sex with a thirteen-year-old girl. "[H]as any other world-class director lived a life so overbrimmingly packed with lurid incident and accident?" [*Vermeer in Bosnia*, (2004)] Weschsler suggests this experience especially equips Polanski to depict atrocity, his subject. But there is also a note of amazement in Weschsler's voice, as if the load of awfulness in Polanski's story is generally unusual and in its heft almost show-offy.

It wouldn't seem so if the qualifier "world-class director" was replaced by "nineteenth century Chinese peasant," or "American slave," or "unmarried, sexually-active female in an Islamic fundamentalist society." To think of Polanski's life as extraordinarily unprotected—although it may be for a film director—you have to forget that most people who ever lived endured over-the-top, potboiler existences that outstrip fiction for irony and harshness.

*

In *Stumbling on Happiness,* Daniel Gilbert explains that memory is mostly an improvisation based on a small number of recorded cues rather than the retrieval of stored data. In a similar way, the brain fills in visual ground missing from the eye's blind spot, where the optic nerve swerves off to join the brain, and so instead of a black hole in our vision, we perceive a seamless vista patched together by the mind's hunch that what is proximate to the blind spot extends through it. We know this fact of our physiology, yet each time we see its proof in a visual field experiment, we gasp with astonishment at the mind's trick. Without forgetting, extinction might be our only contemplation.

*

A reporter for the *New York Times* asked Annie Leibovitz why she took photographs of Sontag as she lay dying and after she had died. Leibovitz said, "You know, you don't stop seeing... One doesn't stop framing. It doesn't turn off and on. It's on all the time."

THE CLOCK

January 7, 2019. The other day my friend Perry, who is an actor, said people can change at any moment of life. It's like working on a scene, where you can decide to play it this way instead of that way. You can stop the action and make a different choice. I am drinking tea and eating those little chocolate star cookies from Trader Joe's.

January 11, 2019. The snow is falling upwards. I'm on the fifth floor, and the enormous naked tree outside my window is swaying. It's beautiful and gray. It's the gray of blur through the window of a moving bus or train, the way the beach looks in blizzards: the white of the sky blending with the white of the snow and the white of the sand—without edges.

January 13, 2019. From a notebook entry of 1995: My mother reviews the dinner for her 80th birthday: "It couldn't have been nicer if we'd hired actors to play the parts."

January 14, 2019. Every time you think of asking a woman to justify the way she exists in her body or spends her money, direct the question to a man and keep doing that for the rest of your life.

January 22, 2019. From a notebook entry in 1996: I ran into P, whom I have recently dreamed about. He's back in my fantasy life now that T and I are no longer seeing each other. I congratulated him on his new book. He launched into a denunciation of the review of it in *The Nation*. I was placed in the role of the listener as he beamed a sort of approval at me. He said he was amazed at the bold way I revealed my sexual self on the page. I wasn't sure I did that and felt a little embarrassed. I envy his confidence. I wouldn't like to be around him too much, unless we were having sex, and I don't want to have sex with him.

January 23, 2019. Every time I see the word SCOTUS, I see the word Scrotus.

January 24, 2019. Dear Male Humans, Please don't let the pain of your individual existences harden you against female resistance. The pain of your individual existence is the pain of all human existence in relationship to people who want things, and to institutions that control you, and to the memory of your own looming extinction. You suffer in intimate life with females who raise you and against whom you often feel small. You feel uneasy when we report the insults that rain down on us, and the double standard of "men can and women can't" that is our condition. We report the ways it feels to be in this position and the toll of living in societies that protect men from awareness of their privilege and slip them past penalties for harms they commit.

You say you are shocked. You are not shocked. You are ashamed, and often people turn against the source of unwelcome consciousness rather than open themselves to the possibility of complicity. If you have been any kind of male human, you have gotten away with shit. You know it, and we know it.

You don't want to be blamed. Plus, your friends are being picked off, one at a time, some with merit, you admit, some as targets of what you call a vigilante tide you sometimes argue disqualifies the entire campaign of justice-seeking. Stop doing that. You feel fucked by the governmental coup we are living under, as do we feel fucked by it, and this feeling of being fucked can go two ways. It can stir your identification with people who feel fucked all the time, including by your cluelessness to our social circumstances. You can say, okay, I wouldn't like that at all. I would really find that awful and although I am not going to help you get the things you want, at least I won't deny the truth of your account. Or you can be a dick and go on being a dick with a bad taste in your mouth nothing will dissolve.

January 30, 2019. No one needs to justify an abortion by explaining the difficulty of the decision or making sure to add you want children, really, just when you're ready. You don't have to want children, ever.

February 9, 2019. I made a meatloaf I've eaten half of. It's a Trader Joe's meatloaf. One pound of the hamburger that is twenty per cent fat. You need the fat. One container of mirepoix. One jumbo egg. If you are a normal person or not female, you might want to chop up bits of very delicious bread and add that. Tons of cayenne and crunchy salt, as many fresh herbs as you have and want to throw in, any other leftovers you can chop finely enough so they will be engulfed by meatloafness. Squish all this together with your hands and form into a football shape in a pan. Slather on tons of Heinz ketchup. You can't use Trader Joe's ketchup. You just can't. Forget about it. Spread the ketchup evenly around the top surface. Bake at around 400 degrees for as long as it takes in your oven. When things begin to brown, you're probably close. Try not to eat it while it's still hot. Don't burn your mouth too badly.

February 9, 2019. A notebook entry from June 1997: I was attracted to a man who was an addict and was unreliable in other ways. My shrink said, "He's afraid he'll do something or want to do something that will wind up sliming you and that will fill him with self-hatred." I thought he just wasn't attracted to me, but I loved my shrink for coming up with this understanding.

February 10, 2019. Albert Finney has died, a beautiful man who fled his beauty the way Brando fled his. The extraordinary beauty of beautiful men who cannot stand being beautiful. After he was no longer beautiful, Finney disappeared into characters it was compelling to watch. When he was beautiful, he was sexy, especially in *Two for the Road*. What makes a person sexy? Maybe the way they seem to be saying: Touch me. It's okay. I want it. And to communicate as well: I am dying to melt into you.

February 19, 2019. I was walking across 93rd Street, on my way to yoga, when I came upon two large bags of books spilling onto the sidewalk. I picked out five, gave away two, and brought three home. One was *A Sorrow Beyond Dreams*, by Peter Handke, written in the early 1970s after the suicide of his mother. The copy I picked up was published in 2002 with an introduction by Jeffrey Eugenides.

The introduction is smashing, sentence after sentence of blistering literary criticism, tender and probing of Handke's clinical restraint in the narrative and of the impossibility of language to represent certain states of feeling and knowledge. Near the end he talks about the particularity of German "void-obsessed" gloom, referencing Goethe, and then, punching through to the heart and counter-heart of his subject, he notes the susceptibility of this gloom to caricature. As an example, he recalls a brilliant moment from *Saturday Night Live*: "Think of Mike Myers as the angular, alienated Dieter of *Sprockets*, sourly twisting his face behind Bauhaus eyewear to say: 'Tell me, in your film, *Irritant Number 4*, the only two images were a baby's head and a toilet. Did you mean for me to scream?'"

February 26, 2019. If another body creates anxiety in you, how about you treat your anxiety instead of referring to the other body? Any size, any concept of beauty, any color parts, any gender or genderfuck, any nakedness, any clothes.

February 26, 2019. Taking issue with comments in Moira Donegan's review in *Bookforum* of Andrea Dworkin's *Last Days at Hot Slit*. The writings of Andrea Dworkin are making a comeback amid the merging of sex-panic and weasel-slaying. Donegan writes: "In time, third-wave sex positivity became as strident and incurious in its promotion of all aspects of sexual culture as the anti-porn feminists were in their condemnation of sexual practices under patriarchy. The movement has spent the past three decades in a state of confusion, unable to reconcile its twin mandates of celebrating women's sexual agency and combating men's sexual violence. Consent has turned into a political divider, separating the parts of our sex lives that should be the subject of feminist analysis from those that should be exempt from political inquiry—what intimacies, pleasures, and pains can be analyzed, and what must be set aside behind a velvet rope. It should not be hard to say that even though women make their own choices with regard to sex, we make those choices under unfairly constrained circumstances; that even though we can and do initiate and enjoy sex, we are also more vulnerable to sexual coercion, exploitation, and violence than men are—and that when we experience these abuses, it is usually at men's hands. It should not be hard to say that heterosexuality as it is practiced is a raw deal for women and that much pornography eroticizes the contempt of women. It should not be hard to say any of this. But it has become hard."

Here, as in a recent piece by Michelle Goldberg in the *New York Times*, promoting sexual freedom is equated with "libertinism," a word Goldberg uses. Libertinism is supposed to be something you wake up from and think is a drunken mistake. "Strident" and "incurious"? Not apparent to me. Nor is anyone saying sex practices, sex fantasies, and reports of what's felt and thought in bed are out of bounds or not part of sexual politics. Where are these velvet ropes? Of course the personal is political. Has there been pressure on women to say it was good when it wasn't good? Sure. But the whole project of consciousness-raising and its later revelations have been to name those kinds of pressures and encourage women to say, in effect: It wasn't good, it was meh, here's what I like.

The idea that consent isn't consent under patriarchy is pure Dworkin, in that things in her understandings are all this or all that. Males and females become essentialized in this warfare model. There is so much pressure in the statement above to brand as traitors, dupes, and manipulated cyphers women who feel any sort of pleasure doing anything with men. While it's true consent is not always consent and pleasure is sometimes faked, it is also true that women are super capable—and increasingly so because of feminism—of telling men to back off when they don't want to do something.

Men are not a monolith. There isn't such a thing as a male libido, a male way of doing sex that is essential and universal to male humans and categorically different from the ways women and other non-males have and think about sex. It is also the case that male humans in pretty substantial numbers commit violent acts against women. How come? Well, religions and other respected cultural practices teach men to devalue women and feel entitled to control their bodies and lives far more diligently than pornography. I think the word "empowerment" is sad in that it means its opposite. Women need to be free not only from the pressures of men and patriarchal culture but also from the projections of other women. Women don't know what women are any more than anyone else knows.

February 27, 2019. A note on Sontag's "The Pornographic Imagination" (1967) in the context of Dworkin: The Undead and the good-girl-itis coloring #MeToo rhetoric. It's easy to turn your nose up at sex if you do it without liking it, and there is lots of pressure to do it without liking it. Sex is messy in the bodily sense and in the emotional sense. It just is. But please don't use feminism as a justification for abstinence. Feminism is not a convent, or a hide-out, or an island of safety. Feminism is the place to go for better orgasms and learning to say, "That doesn't turn me on, this does." Feminism is a strap-on that makes risk easier to bear, including the risks of opposing sexual violence and other forms of violence against women.

Sontag questions what she sees as a ruling liberal assumption that human sexual appetite is "a natural pleasant function" if untampered with by religion and morality, a line of thought that travels from Nietzsche to Freud. She hitches her wagon to the French tradition represented by Sade, Lautréamont, Bataille, and the authors of *Story of O* and *The Image*. She winds up creating her own heavy-breathing and sootily glamorous counter-mythology, but clearly she was excited by who she was fucking at the time.

Story of O chronicles a woman's willing and pleasurable progress toward enslavement and self annihilation. *Story of the Eye* portrays wildly abandoned sex—mostly between a man and two women—involving all the body's effluvia as well as eggs, eyeballs, and the sun, which are versions of the same, obsession-triggering symbol.

In these works, Sontag sees a truer version of sex than the dominant Freudian one, where sex is categorized into forms of pathology bred by Western Christian thought and where sex is imagined, at least in the clinical practice of psychoanalysis, as something that can be fixed. Sontag suggests, following Bataille, that sex is not corrupted by neurosis but is deeper than neurosis, a behavior closer to the warring of chimps and the rutting of bonobos than to most other human activities. She thinks sex is dangerous and difficult to wrap our minds around.

The work of these writers "suggests that 'the obscene' is a primal notion of human consciousness, something much more profound than the backwash of a sick society's aversion to the body. Human sexuality is, quite apart from Christian repressions, a highly questionable phenomenon, and belongs, at least potentially, among the extreme rather than ordinary experiences of humanity. Tamed as it may be, sexuality remains one of the demonic forces in human consciousness—pushing us at intervals close to taboo and dangerous desires, which range from the impulse to commit sudden and arbitrary violence upon another person to the voluptuous yearning for the extinction of one's own consciousness, for death itself. Even on the level of simple physical sensation and mood, making love surely resembles having an epileptic fit at least as much, if not more, than it does eating a meal or conversing with someone. Everyone has felt (at least in fantasy) the erotic glamour of physical cruelty and an erotic lure in things that are vile and repulsive. These phenomena form part of the spectrum of sexuality, and if they are not to be written off as mere neurotic aberrations, the picture looks different from one promoted by enlightened public opinion, and less simple.

"…(Religion is probably, after sex, the second oldest resource which human beings have available to them for blowing their minds. Yet among the multitudes of the pious, the number who have ventured very far into that state of consciousness must be fairly small…) There is, demonstrably, something incorrectly designed and potentially disorienting in the human sexual capacity—at least in the capacities of man-in-civilization. Man, the sick animal, bears within him an appetite which can drive him mad. Such is the understanding of sexuality—as something beyond good and evil, beyond love, beyond sanity; as a resource for ordeal and for breaking through the limits of consciousness—that informs the French literary canon I've been discussing." (in *Styles of Radical Will.*)

February 28, 2019. When you talk about porn, regardless of what you say about porn, it would help to situate us in reality if you acknowledged the porn stash in your head.

March 6, 2019. I watched the first part of the Michael Jackson documentary, *Leaving Neverland* (HBO), about the experiences as boys of Wade Robson and James Safechuck. Everything they said rang true: the sense of romance and excitement the boys felt, their anguish at being replaced, the kind of sexual acts they performed, their feelings about them, their ambivalence about experiences that shaped their lives and about the love Michael aroused in them and appeared to feel for them. The seduction of the parents as well.

We all lie to ourselves for different reasons at different times. The tone in both men of continued wonder and grief and a desire not to erase their experience with only rage and blame. You feel they feel everything. It was allowed to happen the same way all people in power get their way. Priests, teachers, shrinks, the rich, the famous. When you listen to Michael's music and watch him perform, will you think about the revelations of these men? I should think it would be impossible not to. How that will color your reactions is individual. Can we keep complexity in the picture without shaving off some part of reality? The first part of the documentary asks us to do this.

March 9, 2019. *Leaving Neverland,* Part 2, is extraordinary and moving. Wade Robson and James Safechuck are present and touching, grappling with the complexity of their childhoods and the legacy of those experiences in their adult lives. Wade's mother asks, "How could you not have told me?" It was the question my sister asked me about the sexual abuse I experienced at the hands of a man trusted and revered by my family.

I was fourteen. My cousin, to whom it also happened, was eleven when this man began to have sex with her. It happened to me twice in the course of a day and night. That's all, and yet it marked my life. The person doing it to you has no idea how they are changing you from that time forward. You are never going to be the person you were, but this is only something I can tell you looking back over many decades. My sense of myself and the world was spliced that day. At the time, it never occurred to me to tell anyone, just as it did not occur to Wade and Jimmy to tell anyone about their sexual experiences with Michael Jackson, even after other boys came forward. It is part of the enchantment of the experience that you live with it inside you in ways that are not translatable.

The documentary conveys this beautifully in the attention it pays to the men, ushered to sex before they had words for these states of being, and in the way it expresses less interest in blaming Jackson or the parents. I was older and could attach language to my experience. Also, I was not seduced and did not love the man, as Jimmy and Wade loved Michael. I knew all sorts of things I could not speak about. The film is important in tracing the natural history of sexual abuse inside the people it happens to, inside the families that allow it to occur, inside the culture that accepts the limitless power of certain individuals.

So often in stories about sexual abuse, the focus is on the abuser, so people can aim their righteous disapproval without having to take in the more nuanced and layered story of the person who came under the influence of power. What does it feel like being a child with the potential to upend the reality of everyone you know? That condition alone has enormous weight in your psyche, especially if it is unable to be shared. When I wrote about *The Incest Diary,* I encountered the same wish to shift focus to the bad man away from the female narrator who was taking pains to present the moment-to-moment variability of her consciousness. Some people found that too difficult to look at.

I find the accounts of these men riveting because what happened to them and who they were in those moments with Michael contain components that will remain mysterious and unanalyzable.

March 13, 2019. The first act of rebellion is being oneself.

March 18, 2019. Kate Manne, a feminist philosopher, writes a book called *Down Girl: the Logic of Misogyny*. The book reaches the desk of *London Review of Books*, which is edited by a woman, Mary-Kay Wilmers. Most of the other editors are female, and individually or together they assign the review to Adam Phillips, a well-known psychoanalyst and writer who brings a psychoanalytic perspective to what he says. Reading his review, you learn that Manne has no interest in psychoanalytic understandings of women-hate. She doesn't think misogyny is "a property of individual misogynists." She thinks it's a cultural practice. It's not something people are. It's something people do.

This is Phillips's summary, although you don't get to know what Manne thinks about anything until you are a third of the way through his essay. For nearly four columns, he tells you how psychoanalysts understand why people dump on women—in his understanding because of the way they are raised by mothers or not raised by them in certain ways. We learn what Phillips studied when he was at school. In other words, we are told in detail precisely the reasoning Manne disregards.

She's on the front line of misogyny, observing the ways it's so natural in the culture that, for example, the female editors of a prestigious literary journal perform it in their assignments. Phillips kind of mansplains and kind of doesn't. He presents Manne's view of male entitlement as the thing that relies on female humans for "nurturing, comfort, care, and sexual, emotional and reproductive labour." The asymmetry of these relations causes women to try and work out what men want and give it to them. In the process, they give themselves away.

There's tons more rigorous reasoning in the book. Does Phillips do it justice? He does. Ish. But why does it matter to anyone what a male writer thinks about a book about misogyny? Why does Manne need his imprimatur in the minds of the female editors? It's not a freedom-of-expression move, a move in favor of equality and de-essentializing the sexes, a move rejecting gate-keepers and the policing of who gets to speak about what and who owns a topic. The assignment doesn't smell like any of these things. It smells like girls trying to look like they respect the views of men because in the reign of feminist hegemony, men are at risk of being silenced.

March 19, 2019. I saw Claire Danes on Broadway in front of the barbecue place. She looked beautiful, talking to a woman who was shorter than she was, her head moving in that frisky-horse way she has. She was the most beautiful person on the block between 97th and 98th Streets. No one was even close. Everything looked better because she was there. For a fraction of a second, I thought she was someone I knew because I recognized her, and I almost called out hello. I was pulling a suitcase. I wondered whether she lived in the neighborhood and if the ribs in the picture outside the barbecue place tasted as good as they looked.

March 29, 2019. We are packing up our house in Arizona. Richard is giving a talk in a museum. He is wondering if museums might become institutions that de-accession objects. He thinks about the ineluctable bond humans have formed with objects since becoming agricultural beings, 12,000 or so years ago. I am sitting on the couch, one of four pieces of furniture we have left to sell.

I remember the people from whom we bought the things we are selling, and I will remember the people who have come to our house the last few days to transport these things to their new homes. I saw an obit today, offering consolation in that the woman had had a life well spent. I didn't think there was consolation in imagining how a life will play in retrospect.

April 14, 2019. From Peter Schjeldahl's review of the paintings of Berthe Morisot in *The New Yorker,* October 2018: "I am not alone in having remarked that most of our present, really engaged young painters are women. It stands to reason. Men have held forth at relative liberty for a few thousand years. They may continue to impress, but they are considerably less likely to surprise than a class of creators whose testimony, with exceptions mainly in literature, has tended to be patronized even when heeded. Let all canons fall until we have this imbroglio sorted out. How does the past century and a half of art register if, as an experiment, we set Berthe Morisot at center stage and look around from there. I think she can handle it."

I'm struck here by the aesthetic underpinnings of Schjeldahl's call for gender equality. It has to come from this impulse for real change to occur. He's not claiming turnabout is fair play. The male critic has grown bored by the work men make because of the limits on men of being men. It's a response to the glut of one-voiceness, in this case in terms of gender, as we all feel it in terms of other monolithic expressions in art, such as whiteness.

April 20, 2019. I love *Better Things* in its post-Louis C.K. iteration. I love the great splash of shows without plots about people who do not live lives with plots, played by actors who are sad and rueful and comic and crazied by existence amid the thing that is happening to our country. These shows include: *High Maintenance, SMILF, Broad City* (Farewell! Oh, god, the end of the last episode with that parade of alternative, soul-mate Abbis and Alanas talking about everything and nothing with passionate attention to each other). There are other shows I would place in this group. I'm in a packing-cleaning-selling mind-set.

Better Things continues to make brilliant use of Celia Imrie as Phil. In a sense, the show takes place in her mind, which is fraying. Inside dementia-lite she can say and do anything with the freedom of the snobbish, childish, British, disappointed, hateful and lovable creature she is. She's the id puppet for the other characters who are more restrained by a sense of social responsibility. The art of this show is not to point the mess somewhere. It's a letter without a specific reader.

I have to pack more boxes. Richard wants us to pack the moving pod by ourselves. I said, "Why?" He said, "Because I don't know how I want to pack it until I'm doing it, and I don't want other people doing it in a way I won't like." I said, "And you want me to be the carrier mouse?" He said, "Yes."

May 7, 2019. On the subject of likability in women, there is only one issue: Is she willing to give herself away for the sake of others, is she willing to lie about what she wants, who she is, and how she really feels? Likability in men? Not an issue. No one cares.

May 13, 2019. No one should be forced to carry any unwanted pregnancy to term, raped or not. Believing in exceptions is acceding to the framework of restriction. It also shifts the focus from a woman deciding for herself to the state deciding for her. When people focus on girls and women who are raped being forced, it supports a framework in which there is tolerable forcing and intolerable forcing. If abortion rights are not at the top of your political priorities, go fuck yourself.

May 14, 2019. The first time I had sex, the condom broke and I thought my life was over. My mother had a friend who didn't have children. She said of this friend, "She's like a dried-up tree that's never borne fruit." Another time my mother said, "I never wanted children, if anyone had asked me, which they didn't." When my sister was dying she said, "Why didn't you have children?" I said, "I didn't want them." She said, "Does that mean you're selfish?" Look how often women fall out because some have had children and some have not.

May 15 2019. It's 1967, and I'm out with a group picketing abortion hearings in lower Manhattan because women who have actually had abortions are barred from testifying. A reporter from the *Midday* TV show invites us to the studio, and we stand in front of a TV camera in our coats. We stand in a row, like a lineup of criminals, and we answer questions about our movement. Afterward we eat hamburgers, and I walk across the park with Flo Kennedy. In her apartment, she warms up pea soup she has cooked with a ham bone. Near where she lives, in Harlem, a salon applies eyelashes one hair at a time.

May 18, 2019. "The poet John Berryman groped a student in the back seat of a car, en route to a party, and then balked when she tried to brush him off. ('What? You mean you don't fuck?')."—from "Unfinished Work, How sexism and machismo shaped a prestigious writing program," (the Iowa Writers' Workshop) by Maggie Doherty, April 24, 2019, *The New Republic*. I love this anecdote because it encapsulates the lightning way a rejected male human can top his prey with the accusation, "prude." If you don't want to fuck me, there is something wrong with you. Reader, we have all been the girl in the back seat, and this experience is at the core of everything we need to burn down.

May 25, 2019. I found a packet of cigarettes on the street and tilted back the lid. There they were, twelve soldiers lined up in white suits. They smelled good. Richard and I were on the phone. I said, "I don't know if I should leave them for someone or throw them away." I like the culture of the streets where people leave and take uneaten food and other things. I like leftovers: things too good to finish or waiting by the road for a ride. I said, "A poor person who would buy them anyway might want these." Richard said, "Put it down." I said, "It's too late for that. I have to make a decision." These days, you don't see many people smoking on the streets.

June 9, 2019. A nail salon under new management sent out coupons for $10 off, and I slipped into a long, narrow space on Broadway. The woman who did my feet wore a tag with the name Amy. All the women wore the same white tops and blue silk pants that were chic for a uniform. I didn't ask her real name. Mechanical hands in the massage chair worked on my back, and I asked if she preferred the new management to the old. She said she did. Her English wasn't good enough to detail why, and I thought words wouldn't be our form of communication, anyway.

It was quiet, and we were mostly alone as she worked on my not-too-terrible feet. When she massaged my toes and calves, I told her it was wonderful. I wanted to say to do it harder but didn't. She was not in her first youth. We both had short, dark hair. While my toes were drying in the toe dryer, she rubbed my shoulders and neck, and I didn't want anything other than the moment. Not even for it to extend. I gave her a $10 tip. She said, "Why?" I said, "I like you."

July 9, 2019. We're in Amsterdam, and Richard says, "Why do you post pictures of our trip?" I say, "I like to." He says, "Does anyone care?" I say, "No one cares about the fun we are having." He says, "That Porsche is going the wrong way on a one-way street. It just pulled into the garage that charges 60 euros a day." I say, "Banksy doesn't hold up compared to Basquiat and Keith Haring, even the things he created to be exhibited in a gallery space." Richard says, "My sister told me my father had been to Dachau during the war. I wonder why I don't remember him telling me about it. Maybe I was too young when I heard the word Dachau." I say, "People here smile easily and push you aside on the street." Richard says, "I can't eat any more of this cake until we walk." I say, "Walking up to our rooms is like climbing a mountain." He says, "Val was supposed to tell me what my father said to her, but we didn't get the chance to continue the conversation. I wonder why I care so much about his experiences in concentration camps." I say, "You have spent a lot of your life with Jews." He says, "Do you think I did it on purpose?" I say, "People have feelings about Jews as a thing, apart from specific people who are Jews." He says, "I want to find that outdoor market we went to yesterday, the one with old books." I say, "You don't feel the presence of police or other uniformed personnel here. It's a clock that runs by itself." Richard says, "Even children here speak English grammatically." I say, "Bob Dylan is a deeply creative artist." Richard says, "I think seeing concentration camps changed my father's life from that time forward." I say, "Do you think the mouse will come back tonight?" He says, "When Joni Mitchell sings 'Coyote', she makes it sound like the thoughts you have while driving a car." I say,

"When Joan Baez says to Dylan, 'Do you like my dress?' he ignores her." Richard says, "I'll put a towel under the door so the mouse can't get into our room." I say, "Dylan is a zero as a person. He has no personality. He's only alive when he's on stage and doesn't have to give anything personal to anyone." Richard says, "Watch out for that bike! You really have to look before you cross."

July 10. 2019. The thong on my flip-flop broke. We were on a small side street in Amsterdam. I thought I could sew it to the sole well enough to walk if I could find a needle and thread. I went into a shop, and a young man directed me to an outdoor market. I was walking with one bare foot and the other in a flip-flop. The streets are cobbled with small square stones and pour into the canals. I'm afraid of the end of fun. In the market, Richard spotted Chinese shoes with plastic soles and cloth tops. A Dutch woman with high cheekbones and tan skin was wearing them, too. I bought a pair and wore one Chinese shoe and one thong, which had better arch support. Later we found a sewing kit in a store, and I sat on a granite bench and sewed back the thong. It took a long time. I felt like Geppetto.

Anne Frank did not take her diary with her when she was arrested. She must have known it would have a better chance of surviving than she did. She knew she had written a book, and she knew she had a subject: life in hiding. Out of the 140,000 Jews in the Netherlands before the war, 17,000 survived, most of them in hiding. Some did not hide and passed as non-Jews. After the war, when Jews returned to the Netherlands from concentration camps, some Dutch people said to them, "You should be glad you missed what happened to us. We were starving."

A third of the Jews in hiding, including the Franks, were betrayed by Dutch citizens who were not compelled by the Germans to report anything. In 1968, Otto Frank, the sole surviving member of his family wrote, "After the Allies had landed in Normandy in June 1944, we believed we'd soon be liberated. So the shock was even greater when the Gestapo unexpectedly forced their way into our hiding place on 4 August 1944 and arrested us." During the day, those in hiding slept or kept still. No one could use the bathroom, lest they be heard in the shop below. The Franks and the other Jews in hiding were arrested not for doing anything but for being what they were. If tourism isn't interested in the dark side of society, what is it asking us to look at?

July 15, 2019. A response to the flak aimed at Dale Peck's piece about Pete Buttigieg, "My Mayor Pete Problem," (*The New Republic*, July 13). He called Buttigieg "Mary Pete," a play on Mayor Pete, and people are saying this is so homophobic he should be removed from his teaching job at New School. In a cowardly move, *The New Republic* immediately caved and deleted the piece. People: Enough with the finger wagging and the "calling out." It's so boring, you are killing the desire to engage in anything that doesn't pass the purity test. The impulse to reform operates on the conversion model, which has a brilliant history of not working unless you join a cult.

We are all going to die, and knowledge of death is at the core of unhappiness. Whatever happiness is possible in the face of certain death comes from not lying about what is really going on inside us. It comes from using your own words with all the ragged threads hanging off.

July 15, 2019. One night in Amsterdam we went to a splintery pub known as a writers' bar. A row of small tables was lined up in front of a long bench, and near us on the bench a slender young man was reading a book. When the bartender brought him a cake to eat, I said, "What's that?" and he told me, and he told me what else was good to order, and we started to talk.

He said he had stopped using social media, finding it invasive and consuming and perhaps idiotic. I said, "I like addictions." He was English and had started a small press. He'd just published a volume of poems written by Hölderlin, translated by Christopher Middleton. I recalled that Hölderlin had been important to Sebald, and it turned out the young man had also published an essay Sebald had written about Peter Handke.

I said I'd recently read Handke's book about his mother, *A Sorrow Beyond Dreams,* and we talked about a spectacular essay Sebald had written about Handke's play *Kaspar Hauser,* concerning the pain of acquiring language—always freighted with a set of understandings that are received before we can evaluate them. What we talked about matters less than the sense of threads drawing wanderers together.

The threads concerned a Europe still visible on the old streets of the cities where we were walking but emotionally washed out with tides of modern life the young man was perhaps trying to resist. He didn't watch much TV but had seen *The Wire* twice. I said, "Why twice?" He said, "It was a great work of art." I bought him a glass of wine. The next day he brought two of the books he had published to the house where we were staying.

In the bar, he had been wearing a baseball cap. When he took it off, thick, beautiful hair sprang out, and he became a different person.

July 16, 2019. The refreshing thing about Hitchcock's movies is everyone feels guilty. Richard uses an app that tells him ahead of time what mail will be delivered. Not everyone needs a theory to practice sado-masochism. I was aware suddenly that my usual state of unawareness of myself among others was a thing. I was a type. I feel this on the subway. Every time I leave, the plants suffer. In *Mad Men,* Don Draper is told he is beautiful in every episode, a beautiful animal, dazzling, as handsome as a movie star, and he takes it in stride because it has given him his life, the way beauty gives some women their lives.

Things were going well until the A train stopped between stations for an hour. We were on our way back from Europe. We were like mail from the future, and we'd picked up the six hours we'd left behind like a deposit. We had to get out of the train. On Jay Street and Willoughby we shared a Lyft with a stranger who turned out to have friends in common. The handle of my suitcase got bashed, and my head hurt like a hangover, which I might have had, due to a tiny gin and tonic on the plane. All in all, there was nothing to complain about.

July 18, 2019. We are in upstate New York, beginning our search for a house, and this morning Richard talked about Foucault because he is reading volume one of *A History of Sexuality*. He was interested in the way, historically in Europe at least, the subject of sex shifted in the nineteenth century from performing acts of sex to talking about acts of sex, from deeds to conversations, as in the advent of psychoanalysis as a secular form of confession. Still, the contemplation was of sex acts, and he began to think about how, in our current state of sex-panic, the emphasis has shifted to the person who acts and to controlling not only the actor's circulation in the public sphere but also everything the actor has ever touched, all they have produced, even retroactively, an incremental expansion of the range of things that must be removed from circulation, as if their contaminating acts could infiltrate the backward passage of time as well.

During our last night in Amsterdam, we had dinner with two young brilliant women, and one of them, a writer, asked me if, now, you could write anything about *Rosemary's Baby*, which I had been doing, without discussing Polanski's sex crime in 1979, eleven years after the film premiered in 1968. In the interim, Samantha Geimer, the girl with whom Polanski had had sex, has said she was almost fourteen at the time and that she was not as traumatized by what happened as has been claimed. She has asked US courts to drop the charges against Polanski. I said to our dinner companion, "Yes, you can talk about just the movie. I had done it," and she smiled.

July 19, 2019. When Richard enters a memorial museum, a site of conscience, or any museum rooted in an historical period, he thinks about the conversation—or absence of one—the institution is having with the present time and space. In Amsterdam, owing to our friend Enid Futterman, we were invited to meet Jan Erik Dubbelman, International Director of The Anne Frank House, who spoke with us about Anne's evolving significance and the contact zones her story establishes around the world.

Who is in hiding now, and how do they survive? In the rooms we were shown, some available only to those invited behind the velvet ropes, we thought about the conditions that Anne, her family, and the other two families lived in for more than two years before their hiding place was discovered by the Gestapo and they were all—except for Anne's father, Otto—killed in concentration camps. Jan Erik said, "Listen," and we could hear the footsteps of visitors above us and imagine being still and quiet for all the hours of daylight, lest a floor creak and someone downstairs was alerted to the presence of people in hiding.

Anne's face is everywhere on the walls. Her father liked taking pictures of her and her older sister Margot. Teenage girls line up outside. More teenage girls come here than visit any museum anywhere. They come to see where Anne hid and think about the fights they are having with their own mothers. Or they come to discover what significance their lives might have. Anne was fifteen when she was arrested. All over the US now Anne Franks are in camps and in hiding, not for being Jews but yes for being Jews in the broader sense of what Nazi history and the long tale of global anti-Semitism have made the word "Jew" represent: a person who, for no reason other than their existence, is hated and hunted.

When we first met Jan Erik and he took us to the gardens behind the house, my eyes filled with tears imagining this brilliant girl, aware that she and her furious ambition would soon be extinguished. Later, having coffee with Jan Erik in the museum's café, I thought about a joke I loved and I thought Anne would have laughed at if her life had continued, a joke about New York real estate that had special vibrancy in the context of the rooms we had just seen, a form of comedy that makes life bearable to live, given what we know about the horrors humans exact on one another. It was a joke told by Frank Maya, who was one of the first openly gay performance artists on the New York Downtown scene in the '80s and '90s and who died of AIDS in 1995 at age 45. Weighing in on the housing crunch in the city, he says, "Searching for a place in New York really fucks you up. I was watching *The Diary of Anne Frank* on TV last night, and I thought, What a great apartment...the skylight, the bookcase that moves."

July 21, 2019. Two years ago today my sister awoke to her last day. She could speak in the morning, something about love or envy. She was always there. Two years isn't long except in relationship to the time I have left. It's hot today. It feels like Arizona although we are in Hudson. We have met a real estate broker, who showed us a house he owns with his lover. The building had once been a mill and looks out over a rushing waterfall. The house was very beautiful, rough, white, splintery, abandoned, waiting, and inside it all the pressure we had been feeling about the flip-minded suburban houses we had seen plunked amid sparse trees lifted off us. We could picture a house that looked the way we looked to ourselves, although this one was not for sale.

My sister was pale and could just mouth words that morning. Other than that she was dying, she was still there. I already knew the size of the hole she would leave. For a while after she died, she was with me all the time the way she had been with me throughout childhood. Today grief is the color of a grasshopper with light shining through the membranes. When someone dies, I first want their things. That quiets down, except the loss of my mother's ring, stolen from her hospital room, which will never quiet down. I made my sister laugh.

I was happy stretched out beside her on her bed. I have seldom had a job that served a purpose. The days she was dying, I was sleeping in a room that was hot, and I would slip down to the living room, where the air conditioning worked better and where from the couch I could see the baby grand piano that had sat in our parents' house. My mother had learned to play it well. I had been surprised she could focus that well on anything. There on our suburban street, smelling of low tide in the mornings and high tide at night, rose up my mother's secret life, and I had wondered what else she could master if she could play Beethoven that well.

July 25, 2019. On November 8, 2016, the US experienced a fascist coup. Hillary didn't lose the election. There was no election. All the sentences spilled in the interim explain nothing, reveal nothing, express nothing true about what has happened and why it happened. The analysis is sawdust and unreadable. There are no distractions. What is big to me in a frame may be trivial to you. I would bet it is. Looking for origins is reverse teleology. The thing you are talking about as a thing is mutating all the time. Even if you knew what caused it, and even if you knew what it was, knowledge of the cause wouldn't fix it. Using the word "president" is obscene. On and on goes the charade. I know nothing more than anyone else, except that anything even remotely governmental in this setting, with these officials, is a charade.

Things that used to feel good on a personal level are saturated with the knowledge of how we are living. Nothing is separate. It never has been. I'm not depressed. These thoughts don't issue from a psychological state. I see massive amounts of cruelty called other things, massive amounts of money spent to hurt and deprive the majority of people and the planet's ecology. I couldn't care less about why this feels good to so many people. The analysis of origins seems irrelevant. Haven't you noticed how pathetically washed out all discussions of Mueller have been for many months? The Right Wing coup is a closed system on a feedback loop with its own power. It doesn't care about demoralizing us. It doesn't have to care. It doesn't feel threatened.

July 31, 2019. Let's say, for argument's sake, his head explodes, and no dogs are harmed by flying fragments of skull. I think the majority of the things that squirm in his wake would deflate. The great bubble of their bodies would lose air, and they would sink back into bland, nameless primordial dread and resentment. They are not a movement. They do not believe in anything. They are moved from point A to point B by money, and algorithms, and bad moons or sick planets, but I think they would go away ish. This is my hope and belief, a kind of sandwich of speculation entirely lacking in data. Data isn't data, anyway.

August 23, 2019. Last night I saw a screening of *Lynch: A History*. About football I know nothing. The thing you feel immediately is the charm of the great running back, Marshawn Lynch, with his dimples and dreads, in the hands of master collagist David Shields. The director applies his skills with jump cuts and montage proximities to the medium of documentary film-making, whence they originated. The effect is different from other films in the way film-brain and text-brain zigzag back and forth. There is a thesis-ish. Shields intends to trace the development of a political consciousness in Lynch that takes the form of refusing to interact with corporate sports media. He won't answer questions because the questions ask him to explain and ingratiate himself. In his eloquent and often comic refusal, he is saying, in effect: I am absent in your view of me, and I'll make a point of showing you what absence looks like. About race and the body of the powerful black man, time's up with the explanations. The film consists of 700 plus rapid-fire clips ripped mostly from the web in fair-use bites. The doc is a poem, and so are the 50-yard and 75-yard broken filled runs Lynch accomplishes in a body that knows where to go and what to do.

IN 1968 I THOUGHT IT WOULD ALWAYS BE 1968

I am thinking about a man I liked who died young. He keeled over one day from a stroke at 38. Nothing could have predicted his end, and I remember the shock of this death, which was like the shock of death itself coming out of nowhere around the wrong turn. I took a class this man taught when I was a graduate student at Columbia. He'd have students over to his apartment near the university, and he had a small child who had been a baby in 1968.

The baby had been standing in his crib, on the verge of saying his first words, when out of his mouth flew the chant, "Irk must ohhh." For a solid week at the end of April 1968, the words "Kirk must go" had risen over the campus, floated into the baby's room, and changed his life evermore. I don't know what happened to the baby, but nothing could erase the fact of his first words and his eager, joyous parroting of the shouts hurled at Grayson Kirk, Columbia's president, who had linked the university to the Defense Department and promoted the construction of a large gym in Harlem that residents of Harlem would be restricted from using.

The shouts had risen up as demonstrators circled the five buildings students were occupying until, on the eighth day, April 30, Kirk called the police and 700 people were arrested. I was part of the human chain surrounding the buildings. We wore black arm bands after the arrests. It was my last year at Barnard and in June we would protest by walking out of our graduation and thundering down the steps of St. John the Divine with our gowns flying behind us.

Earlier that year I had marched in Washington against the war in Vietnam, and the previous year I was present when, on October 21, Jerry Rubin and Abbie Hoffman tried to end the war by levitating the Pentagon. I was married. The man I was married to knew things I did not know, and I liked being swept into his understandings. The marriage was like being swallowed by the wrong whale, the whale of another epoch you would have to swim out of, which I did, being good at the ruthlessness and disloyalty of youth. Grayson Kirk would resign from Columbia before the end of 1969.

I am reading about Valerie Solanas and Ti-Grace Atkinson. The great burst of feminist rebellion I encountered in college was the best thing that happened in my life. Kate Millett is my teacher at Barnard, and I'm at the meeting of NOW where Betty Friedan chastises Ti-Grace, the president of New York NOW, for visiting Valerie in jail. Valerie is in jail for shooting Andy Warhol and the art critic Mario Amaya. Betty doesn't want the women's movement mixed up with the wrong people, even though the wrong people are the only ones who can make the women's movement the women's movement.

I'm excited. I think I am there because Kate likes me. At the meeting, no one is saying Andy Warhol deserved to be shot, although that's what Valerie believed. Not because he had power as a man but because she had gotten it into her head he planned to steal her writing. He had no such plan. Her estimation of her value, seen in the past as a sign she was crazy, can be seen now as a sign she was also prescient.

SCUM Manifesto, written by Valerie in 1967, takes the foundational belief of all cultures and societies—that women are deformed, contaminating agents that need to be tightly controlled and eliminated without conscience—and says the exact same thing about men. In the flash of this reversal, the world is shown how society already works. Valerie's great gift to feminism is unapologetic rage, and Valerie is funny, with her intimate knowledge of contradictions that can't be resolved. On her list of men who need, unequivocally, to be eliminated are: "rapists; politicians...; lousy singers and musicians; Chairmen of Boards; Breadwinners; landlords; owners of greasy spoons and restaurants that play Muzak; 'Great Artists'; ...cops; tycoons...; liars and phonies; disc jockeys; men who intrude themselves in the slightest way on any strange female; real estate men; stock brokers; men who speak when they have nothing to say."

There's a Southern-woman, quiet glamor to the steeliness of Ti-Grace. She's blonde and willowy, and Valerie takes one look at her and sees another parasite wanting a piece of her outlaw fame. It will turn out Ti-Grace hasn't read *SCUM* during the time she promotes Valerie as a hero of feminism. Copies of *SCUM* aren't easy to come by until that August when Maurice Girodias publishes Valerie's book without her permission while she awaits trial at Elmhurst Psychiatric Hospital. Valerie shoots Andy on June 3. On June 4, we walk out of the Columbia graduation. On the morning of June 6, I am sleeping when the phone rings and the man I am married to says, "Kennedy's been shot." He's crying. I think he means John Kennedy, and I don't understand why he's telling me this. He says, "Bobby's dead." Martin Luther King had been killed in April. I don't know if I'm awake or dreaming.

On March 31, worn out by protests against the war in Vietnam, Lyndon Johnson has said on national TV, "I shall not seek and I will not accept the nomination of my party for another term as your President." In a year or so, he will have grown his hair long.

*

2019. I'm in London in a white room. Pillars of books stand in a corner, awaiting boxes. A ladder leans against a wall. Sunlight streams over white couches and lipstick-pink pillows. It looks like a life building up and tearing down at the same time. It looks like my life, as Richard and I consider buying a house outside Hudson, New York. I'm at the home of a new friend, who is moving. We met several years ago on Facebook, the friend of a friend, and last year we met in the flesh, and the way you sometimes feel another person's body in their writing turned out to be accurate in our case. Our lives, made possible by feminism, have sometimes been lived alone, sometimes with intimate partners, always with friends and work at the center of our days. She makes films in a way that is similar to the way I make texts, as a collage of fluid, comic moments modeled after the famous quip of T.S. Eliot: "Plot is the bone you throw the dog while you go in and rob the house."

My friend is not as old as I am but old enough for 1968 to be rich in memory, including the way movies were social necessities as well as art objects and entertainments. We used to see everything the day it opened. Everything from France or Italy or Poland or Japan, sometimes sitting close to the front at the first afternoon screening. These notable movies were released in 1968: *2001: A Space Odyssey, The Killing of Sister George, The Night of the Living Dead, Rosemary's Baby,* and *Barbarella*. I thought I would write here about *2001*. I schlepped an original poster of that movie to Arizona, where I lived when I could with the man I am with now, and schlepped it back to New York when he said goodbye to the Southwest. The poster shows an image of the star baby, a fetus that is also a planet and looks a little like Keir Dullea, who played Dave, the hapless astronaut who is the love object of a computer and who, on Jupiter in the last segment, is exiled to another white room in Stanley Kubrick's brain.

I find myself drawn instead to *Rosemary's Baby,* which emits a constant-now aura more than the other films. *Barbarella* is a spurt at the end of a defunct age of females as instruments of male self-definition. *Rosemary's Baby,* on the other hand, is shot from Rosemary's point of view. Granted, it's a point of view devised by male writers and filmmakers, but Roman Polanski, in his debut American film, identifies both with the weasel husband and the hunted, doomed heroine, and that tension sustains the film more than anything else.

I remember hunkering down in my seat at those films with the expectation of release. Movies were trance states that took you. I had seen and loved the films Polanski had made in Europe: *Repulsion* and *Cul-de-Sac*. I remember the feeling of not understanding certain movies—*Hiroshima, Mon Amour* comes to mind—and believing the fault was in my ignorance and inexperience, which partly it was, and I like remembering the hopefulness in such memories because I believed I would one day acquire the knowledge to understand more, at least in aesthetic terms, and I would turn out to be right. Certain movies and certain paintings and certain books taught you how to see and read in ways you had never imagined before, and they taught you how to see secret layers of meaning and power in the world as well.

Perhaps I've seen *Rosemary's Baby* one time since the original viewing. Certain images remain sharp. Interestingly, they are not of Mia Farrow, who is almost translucent, like a guppy, in the role of Rosemary, the pushed-around wife, who in real life was married to Frank Sinatra in a what-the-fuck move backwards disguised as a rebellious leap. Sinatra would end their marriage after Farrow refused to walk off the set when the picture ran five weeks over schedule.

Much has been written with regard to this film about fears of pregnancy and of the monstrous baby. Those fears remain in the zone of the biological, where it is always comforting to locate women. The horror of the film isn't the Devil or the pregnancy but the marriage. In other words, the horror is social. The pact made by the actor husband to advance his career is not a trade of himself to the Devil but of his wife's body and future. The terms of an ordinary 1960s marriage are presented here as a gothic nightmare.

I remember the men in the movie. The permanent, shit-eating smirk on the face of John Cassavetes, as if he already knows, in a Dantean afterlife, he will be devoured by guilt for eternity. The polished confidence on the shining face of Ralph Bellamy, who plays the vaunted gynecologist, trusted by armies of well-to-do breeders, who is also one of the witches. It is a time when male doctors confer in private with the husbands and fathers of their female patients.

I am rewatching *Mad Men* at the moment, where the shrink treating Betty Draper speaks to her husband Don, who is paying the bills, about Betty's treatment. Betty is another woman sacrificed to the career of her husband, who in this case doesn't do it any more consciously than brushing his teeth or slipping out of his daughter's birthday party. Betty's life in the show isn't understood to have anything to do with her wishes. In *Rosemary's Baby*, the horror shown in scrupulous detail is all the secret deals made by men and some women about the body and life of the married woman, assumed to be in the hands of other people. Her rebellion, too late and in isolation from other women, must fail.

I came of age amid post-war prosperity and before the age of AIDS. I didn't know it was a wormhole in history. Both my parents grew up in families of seven people, crammed into tiny tenement flats. My mother spoke Yiddish until, at age five, she went to school and learned English. My father left school after the ninth grade to sell ladies' dresses in New England. He was too young for a driver's license, so he hired someone to drive him around. Two decades later he had enough money to send his daughter, me, to a private school and then to an Ivy League college, where students believed they could derail a crazily misguided war and make a revolution for women.

During the summer of '68, the Summer of Love, I am cranking up my crafts business that pays for ski trips and meals out. I make colorful jewelry out of plastic bits I buy on Canal Street and out of twisted pieces of vibrant tissue paper I form into shapes with polymer medium. I make paper neckties with psychedelic designs on one side and on the other side personal ads from *The East Village Other*, describing sexual tastes I am curious to know more about. During the Summer of Love, head shops and hippie clothing boutiques throng the streets of the West Village and the East Village, and I carry my wares to these shops, and everyone wants them. Sometimes the man I am married to and I stay up all night making neckties to fill orders. I hang them to dry on a clothesline strung down the length of our apartment. People wear toe rings and finger rings in the shapes of enormous flowers that have a tendency to melt in the rain. I am the least hippie-like and most studious girl Kate Millett has reached out to. Maybe I remind her of herself.

In the fall of '68, I begin graduate school at Columbia and start an affair with a gay boy in my class. His brother knows someone in the administration, and he lives in a mansion, owned by the university and situated on Riverside Drive, as a sort of caretaker. The building has been a school. There are rows of sinks and toilet stalls, and the boy camps out in one room with a mattress on the floor. It's where we have sex after class, and then I ride the subway to the Village where I live. I don't know why I have agreed to marry anyone at nineteen. Something about the man's seriousness has attracted me, but he deserves someone more like him, and in a few years he will marry another woman and live the sort of life I will by then be sure I don't want.

Last night I watched the first four episodes of the six-part series *Years and Years*, a BBC show created by Russell T. Davies. It portrays a future fifteen years ahead that is so close to now it is terrifying in the sense that *Rosemary's Baby* is terrifying, conjuring menace in ordinary life, something brewing in the body, the family, the *polis* that controls us. We follow a British family in which the issues of race and sexuality that ignited the 1960s and decades after have been sorted out. The family easily accommodates its Chinese, black, biracial, and homosexual members.

On the show, a *Dark Mirror* version of technology has eliminated privacy in a way that comforts as much as it suffocates. Any time a family member has a thought or announcement, all the others are patched into a continual Skype and Facetime collectivity. One daughter has decided she's transhuman and has had phone networks implanted in her hand and arm, so her hand works as a phone. This quest isn't shown as a horror, rather it's a variation on long-standing body modifications, including tattoos, piercings, and transexual surgeries. (Remember when the hand of the character played by James Woods in David Cronenberg's 1983 film *Videodrome* is fused with a gun? Remember when, in the most economic jumpcut in film history, Stanley Kubrick's joyous ape tosses the femur he has just used to murder a fellow ape into the air, and it becomes a floating space ship?)

The social fabric comes unglued in the successful marketing of stupidity. Trump has won a second term and has detonated a nuclear device at a man-made Chinese island in the Pacific. Pence has won subsequent terms, and a similar shard of hate-sprewing shrapnel, portrayed by Emma Thompson, becomes Prime Minister of the UK with the aid of CGI-made videos showing her opponents making incendiary statements they never made. People vote for the Thompson character, even though they know the videos are fake. The banks fail. People lose their savings. The North Pole melts. So far in human history, there has been no example of hunter-gatherers going back once they have become agricultural. It has always been assumed to be a one-way door, but now, in the apocalypse that has already occurred, people who have not drowned or burned in unprecedented waves of heat will have no occupation but foraging to survive.

Years and Years is the bleak alternative to the hopes of 1968, not the logical end-point of that arrow. In 1968, we thought everyone in our generation believed in progressive social transformation. We got two presidents to resign. We got a war to end. We got abortion rights. Fifty years later, we got a black person elected as US president. We were wrong about the numbers in our generation who shared our views. Drugs and other diversions took their toll. A year after the raging success of *Rosemary's Baby*, Polanski's wife Sharon Tate, then eight and a half months pregnant, was murdered by the Manson family, a deranged variation on the hippie commune with back-to-nature girls and bearded boys practicing free love.

Looking back, mostly the social transformations we fought for and achieved turned out to be a speck on the great engine of consolidated wealth and the way it could monopolize not only individual societies but the entire world and world history. "Everyone is American," remarks a character in *Years and Years*.

Hudson 2019. I saw a house that was beautiful and empty, and its beauty was in its emptiness. I walked up beautiful stairs, built in the shape of a ramp and crossed floors of gleaming wood and slate tiles, and I looked out the large windows into woods that were quiet except for birdsong, and I wondered if I could live anywhere. I have a friend who, even as a teenager, wanted a house and someone to love her. She has a house and has many times been loved. She didn't know she was beautiful when she was beautiful. I like looking back to a time of jealousy because you remember wanting things deeply and desperately, and you remember a time you were shadowy to yourself. Everything was personal. The way the world worked was personal.

On the flight to England, my feet swelled and lost their customary map of veins and small bones, and when I looked at them I didn't know where I was walking. The other night I walked in my sleep. I walked into the kitchen and pulled all the knives from the wooden knife block onto a cutting board. There they were when I went to make tea in the morning, in a fan shape with the handles dipped in hummus. I had closed the lid on the hummus and put it on the floor with other things I was taking to the airport. My first thought was: A rodent has done this. I tried to picture a rodent large and strong enough to have extracted the knives from the block and restrained enough not to finish the hummus. A close friend once told me we had the same rodenty, Jewish faces, and after that I could see what she meant.

I discovered the knives at 4 am. I had taken an Ambien at twelve something, thinking I would catch a few hours sleep before getting to the airport for an early flight. Have you ever committed an act you were not present at? This happens to Richard, who is a Type 1 diabetic, frequently in periods of extreme low sugar. Sometimes as he slips into a low he can feel it happening, and the slide is pleasurable, like the drug for colonoscopies. I remember having the oddest sense of sleep that felt like a boat rocking, a sense of momentum with flashing images, a boat rocking in a storm. I have never walked in my sleep before. The knives are Henkelses and Wüsthoffs. I bought them from a man who was moving to Hawaii and couldn't take them. I also bought his Breville kettle. In 1968, I thought 1968 would always be 1968, and I couldn't see past that moment.

THE CLOCK

May 16 2019. I am waiting for the light to change on 12th Street. I'm on a little island, and cars are whizzing fast. A young man in a hoodie sidles up close to me and says, "How can I get money off you?" I don't have anywhere to move and say, "No." It's not the answer to his question. There's a little hole in my mouth. A crown has come off at dinner the night before, and I'm on my way to the dentist to get it cemented back on. He stands close and says again, "How can I get money off you?"

I look at him. He's beautiful. There are little tattoos on his face and hands. Blond corkscrew curls tumble out of the hoodie onto his forehead. His skin is the color of caramel, and there's a tribal thing happening with his outfit and jewelry and the whole look of him. I say, "Sweetheart, you're beautiful, and that's no way to start a conversation with a stranger." I'm carrying a yoga mat. A shy smile forms on his face. Maybe he's stoned and isn't sure what's happening. I don't know what's happening. It's his beauty, or the boredom of the way the exchange is supposed to go. Young to old. Tan to white. Male to female. What the fuck ever to what the fuck ever. I say, "Let's start again," and I hold out my hand, and he takes my hand.

HOUSE

I saw a house on Zillow one night at 3 am. I liked the price and that a new, renovated house was inside an old house, built in 1932. Actually, two houses had been smushed together somehow. There are two front doors and two sets of stairs to upper floors that do not connect. On the lawn stands a giant solar panel that revolves and cantilevers toward the sun, supplying most of the energy needed for the house. The renovations were left unfinished, the landscaping left to go to weed.

I was thinking about dogs I could love and dogs I could not love because they don't look like the kind of dogs I imagine loving. The kinds of dogs I could not love include pugs and French bull dogs, with their puzzled brows and snorts of curiosity or who knows what. Then I remembered falling in love with Abigail Cat, who lived in a house we were caring for one winter. She was old and her belly swayed and sagged, and I thought if your wires are hooked up, you can fall in love with anything.

Tomorrow is the memorial for my great feminist friend, and I feel excitement rise about seeing people from the past. It's a quickening of longing that keeps me known to myself. Abraham Maslow invented a hierarchy of needs. At the bottom are food and shelter. Above them are safety and security. At the top is what he called "self-actualization," in which you achieve your full creative potential, whatever that is.

The other day in Hudson the skies were about to open. A man was leaning against the brick wall of a building and invited us into a communal art space he'd established. He said that in a former life he'd been a shrink, and I said I'd had a dream the night before. He asked me to tell it to him. I said, "I was driving our Subaru, and when I got out of the car, I saw that three of the tires were flat. Not only flat. The rubber was in tatters, and the metal had melted." I said I'd awakened at 4 a.m. with thoughts about the basement of the house we are buying and its mysterious machines. The man asked me about my life and I told him my sister had died. He asked if my parents were alive, and I said they were dead. He said, "Those are the three flat tires." I felt something move out toward me from the man's warm eyes. In the dream, I leave the car to get help then can't find it again. Yesterday in NYC, someone was moving out of our building and left a new air conditioner and a new portable heater in the basement, and I took them. The things I want are never mine.

Richard says, "Every house you buy involves a story, often a sad one that has led to its sale." The seller of the house we are buying has a patchy mustache and walks with his hips thrust forward, like a runway model. He doesn't own the house, rather has the rights to sell it. Before the inspection for radon, he left the windows open, although tampering with a property this way is a serious infraction of real estate practice and although radon gas, left undetected, is the second highest cause of cancer in the US. In the light of day, this man no doubt believes it's fair to squeeze all you can from a deal, since the seller has to pay for radon remediation. But at night in his sour dreams, rotting timbers fall from the decaying houses he sells. He can see them sailing to the ground from the broken window he stands before, and he can feel the tremors of the floorboards as he plunges into a pile of rubble. The basement, garage, and shed of the house we are buying are crammed with generations of mildewed furniture and clothes. Inside these boxes, I have eyed things I want.

I am fond of a woman who runs a vintage clothing shop near the house we are buying. She has round cheeks and lively, darting eyes. Today I brought her a box of things I had thinned from my closet, and as I showed her skirts I no longer wear and a pair of suede ankle boots I can't fit over my bunions, my life flashed before me. There was a wrap dress bought for me by a friend after a savage breakup. It's uncanny the way, from the first moments, you can tell who will disappoint you, and yet that knowledge stops no one. The friend who bought me the dress suffered, as I did, more from breakups than deaths. Maybe everyone does. The woman at the vintage clothing store offered me a good price for the clothes, and in the exchange of sad belongings for absence, I loved the emptiness of the rooms awaiting us.

Kathy Acker liked to buy houses and then not live in them. She liked imagining a new life but not being somewhere in particular. If I think of the house we are buying as an art installation called "House," to which we will add "Table" and "Chair," I can see myself happy there. I once spent a month in a tiny house designed by architects and built in an art gallery as part of a project called "Novel." Along with two other writers in similar houses, I was supposed to produce a novel. I did not produce a novel, but I loved being fed and housed alongside other artists. We promised not to leave the premises, and I wondered why anyone thought we would want to.

Since the death of my friend, I have been thinking about the place she occupied in the minds of those who knew her. The minute you become a feminist—and I think it takes a minute—all the language used to describe everything in the world sounds false. It sounds thin and wrong, and what are you going to do? Argue with every word? I would, honestly, but the language of argument is boring to me, so you have to figure out a way to exist in the world that to you is bizarro world, while your world, the world shared by other feminists, is the real world too few people acknowledge. The way to live in bizarro world and not go nuts or waste your existence in rage is what my friend who died gave me a map for—me and every other person who fell under her spell. She said: Come. We will do things and eat something. We will drink something and talk about how to create more space in existence for women, and that is how we will get through life.

The absence of my friend is not the loss of a single person. It's the loss of a wave, a home for the wayward and unanchored, a form of doing politics that is the same as doing the rest of life. She was very smart and funny, and I thought she could see right through whatever falseness was in front of her but didn't have the time to waste on not loving what there was to love.

It's hard to evoke a person everyone likes and values. We remember the rubs and scrapes and twinges in life more than anything because we just do. The absence of my friend is a loss far greater than the loss of one person, just as the persistence of one empty and joyless despot now threatens everything in existence. One person who could love. Another individual who, like a rotting, mildewed box, radiates a misery people want. In the garden of forking paths, I do not meet Richard, and my life is a fly in a jar of honey.

When a man I loved was diagnosed with bone marrow cancer, no one called it a terminal illness. Before my sister died, she said, "Keep me in your pocket when you walk." As long as we keep walking, we don't have to believe the diagnosis. If we don't believe the diagnosis, we can move into the house. You need a place to live while the rot recedes and the world learns to breathe again.

AFTERWORD

by Marco Roth

There's an art to walking around New York City: It's in the rhythm and in the interactions, like dance. Learning to flow is the essential thing, not breaking stride—not getting thrown off stride—but still taking in absolutely everything, or as much as humanly possible. The beauty, the horror, the zaniness; the people doing disgusting things; the variety of things people have made into an art form, like carrying a bagel and two cups of coffee; the dialogue in almost every human language. All these forms of desire are coming at you, shaping the very streets you pace, wrestling and jostling with your thoughts. To those who have learned to truly enjoy walking in New York City, a mental exercise accompanies the physical one: appreciation, articulate ordering, selection, collection, and curation of experience becomes a kind of second nature, but also knowing when to push back and claim one's own space. The other thing you learn is that if you don't want to break stride, you've got to go against the lights and outside the lines. This could also be a description of what used to be called "Criticism."

It should come as no surprise to anyone who's just read the preceding pages that Laurie Stone is one of New York City's most gifted walkers. You've just been out with her. If you're feeling a little breathless, that's to be expected. Laurie is also one of this era's most gifted critical observers. Asking myself why that is, I realized it's because she's unintimidated by the internet.

Spending time online these days can be a lot like walking around New York in the mad, bad, dangerous days of the late 1960s, 1970s, and early 1980s, when Laurie was coming of age and into her own as a writer and critic at *The Village Voice*: Right next to an anarchist encampment, someone is banging a pot and yelling about Jesus, and someone else is collecting donations for the victims of a foreign war, and there are free newspapers everywhere and being used for everything from hats, to bedding, to anonymous ransom notes; a cab driver shouts racist things at a group of kids crossing the street (against the light), construction workers make unprintable comments about passing women, and yet it seems possible, and even likely, that every tenth person you cross is a secret genius. This was the city that I was born too late for (thanks, Rudy Giuliani), but insofar as I can feel my way back there and into its spirit, it's through Laurie. And Laurie's experience of that New York, let's call it "Punk New York" has helped her keep her cool online while so many others have lost theirs. But Laurie's cool isn't about ironic distance or Sontag-like detachment and aloofness. Hers is the cool that comes after cool, when a person has decided to be only one thing: herself, and as much of that and as fearlessly as possible.

What I'm talking about, of course, is freedom. Laurie is probably freer than you—she's freer than me, I know—but she also teaches you how to be free. The right-wing has done as good a job screwing up a word like "Freedom" for the rest of us as they've screwed up everything else. But if we're ever going to recover a sense of liberty for ourselves, to remember what it's like to move, talk, and write without fear, without looking over our shoulders and worrying how we'll read to others when our every move is captured on surveillance cameras, we should all spend more time in the company of Laurie Stone. She's walking here.

ACKNOWLEDGMENTS

Out of the blue I received a message from Steve Mitchell, who said he'd been reading my posts on Facebook and could we talk about doing some kind of book together. He and his partner Brian Lampkin ran a bookstore in Greensboro North Carolina and had started publishing books. I said sure. I hadn't even met him but liked the sound of his voice and easy laugh when we talked on the phone. He came to New York City, and we met in a coffee place that is also a plant store, and I liked looking across the table, framed by giant ferns, at his warm eyes as we talked about our lives as writers and the terrifying shape the world had assumed. I believe we find our comrades in less than a second in the flesh. I'm not always right, but in this case I was. Steve has been a beautifully responsive editor. It has been a pleasure working with him, and the book is better in every way because of his thoughtful suggestions.

The pieces gathered here were formed as collages from Facebook posts, reviews, and notebook entries written from prompts with Richard. Some pieces were written on assignment for the publications *n + 1* and *Women's Review of Books*. I owe huge thanks to the editing brilliance of Marco Roth, Dayna Tortorici, and Jennifer Baumgardner. The piece "In 1968 I Thought It Would Always Be 1968" was written for a forthcoming anthology about that year, edited by Joan Hawkins. "Personal Life" is a collage of mini essays derived from longer pieces I've written over the years that touch on sex and gender. "The Clock" is a Facebook diary, revealing life in a social surround that, even as it happens, remains unimaginable.

I have thousands of friends on Facebook. During the years I spent long stretches in Arizona with Richard, I was lonely and looking for a cocktail party, even an ersatz one. Facebook became that for me. Hundreds of people have commented on the posts included here, and they have all enlarged my thinking as well as my understanding of how to function in a social group. Among this giant number, special thanks is owed: Regan Good, Thomas Bolt, Holly Hughes, John Weir, Marco Roth, Katherine Dieckmann, Sharon Thompson, Richard Toon, Ruth Novaczek, Timothy Schaffert, Brendan Lemon, Diane Seuss, Gordon Beeferman, Dale Peck, Joy Press, Peggy Shaw, Matthew Sharpe, Patricia Horan, Don Shewey, Emily Nussbaum, Emily Carter, Mikhail Iossel, Lara B. Sharp, Abigail Thomas, Mike Mennonno, Chavisa Woods, Michael Klein, Jasmina Jz Sinanovic, Ian Dreiblatt, Val Vinokur, Jincy Willett, Iris Smyles, Frederic Tuten, Joy Garnett, Robert Marshall, Bill Lessard, Alexis Danzig, Judith Podell and Sjohnna Bruce McCray.

Every writer thanks the person they live with. Richard Toon is also the partner I write with and think with and talk to in the bath. So thanks.

My sister Ellen died of metastatic lung cancer during the time these pieces were being written. She read everything I wrote. She said, "Send it to me," no matter the subject or form. I knew I would miss her before she died, but I didn't want to think about how much because I still had her and why muck that up. I held onto even the almost-dead Ellen, who spoke to me the morning of the day she would die. She was lucid. She said something about love and maybe the burden of love? I miss her so much, there are no words.

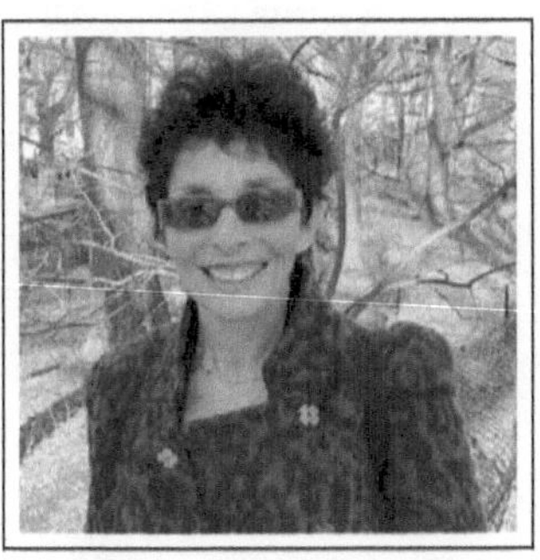

Laurie Stone writes fiction, hybrid literature, and criticism. Her most recent book is *My Life as an Animal, Stories*. She was a longtime writer for *The Village Voice*, theater critic for *The Nation*, and critic-at-large on "Fresh Air." Her writing has appeared in numerous journals including *n + 1*, *Waxwing*, *Tin House*, *Evergreen Review*, *Fence*, *Open City*, *Threepenny Review*, *Women's Review of Books*, and *Creative Nonfiction*. Her website is lauriestonewriter.com.

www.ingramcontent.com/pod-product-compliance
Lightning Source LLC
Chambersburg PA
CBHW032021050726
47590CB00006B/2254

9781732932821